200

CAKES & BAKES

SARA LEWIS

*For Miss Morley, an inspirational
teacher and lifelong friend*

An Hachette UK Company
www.hachette.co.uk

First published in Great Britain in 2008 by Hamlyn,
a division of Octopus Publishing Group Ltd,
Carmelite House, 50 Victoria Embankment,
London EC4Y 0DZ
www.octopusbooks.co.uk

This edition published in 2016

Some of the recipes in this book have previously
appeared in other books published by Hamlyn

Distributed in the US by Hachette Book Group,
1290 Avenue of the Americas, 4th and 5th Floors,
New York, NY 10020

Distributed in Canada by Canadian Manda Group,
664 Annette St., Toronto, Ontario, Canada M6S 2C8

ISBN 978-0-600-63352-5

A CIP catalogue record for this book is available
from the British Library

Printed and bound in China

10 9 8 7 6 5 4 3 2 1

Standard level spoon measurement are used in all recipes.

Eggs should be medium unless otherwise stated. This book
contains dishes made with raw or lightly cooked eggs. It is
prudent for more vulnerable people such as pregnant and
nursing mothers, invalids, the elderly, babies, and young
children to avoid uncooked or lightly cooked dishes made
with eggs. Once prepared these dishes should be kept
refrigerated and used promptly.

Ovens should be preheated to the specific temperature.
If using a convection oven, follow the manufacturer's
instructions for adjusting the time and the temperature.

This book includes dishes made with nuts and nut
derivatives. It is advisable for customers with known allergic
reactions to nuts and nut derivatives and those who may
be potentially vulnerable to these allergies, such as pregnant
and nursing mothers, invalids, the elderly, babies, and
children, to avoid dishes made with nuts and nut oils.
It is also prudent to check the labels of pre-prepared
ingredients for the possible inclusion of nut derivatives.

contents

introduction

introduction

Making your own cakes and cookies is immensely rewarding and relaxing. After a hectic week, making up a batch of cupcakes can be a great therapeutic way to unwind. The wonderful smell of their baking will soon have the family gravitating toward the kitchen, clamoring to eat them before they have had an opportunity to go cold.

Homemade cakes and bakes surpass any store-bought version, no matter how expensive, and are a highly personal way to spoil family and friends. Many of the centerpiece cakes (see pages 134–179), for example, can be adapted for a special birthday with the addition of candles and perhaps a piped chocolate or iced message. Or why not take a batch of homemade small cakes (see pages 14–63) or cookies (see pages 64–107) when visiting friends, instead of a bunch of flowers. If you don't have much time then try the traybakes (see pages 108–133). They are all quick and

easy to assemble and are perfect for taking on picnics or packing into school or office lunchboxes. Many of the cakes can also be served warm so that they double as a dessert when served with custard or ice cream.

With many children no longer doing cooking at school, baking is also a good way of encouraging children to learn to cook. There is no mystique to cake baking and it really isn't as tricky as some people think. Providing you have a reliable set of measures and some basic cake pans, and you follow the recipes accurately, then it really is child's play. In addition, you know exactly what has gone into your own cooking so you can keep artificial flavorings and additives to a minimum. You probably already have many of the ingredients in your pantry, and any specialist ingredients can be added to the cart next time you are in the supermarket.

baking equipment

The recipes in this book are all easy to make and the chances are you will already have most of the basic equipment needed to make them. Any additional items that you need can be bought in your nearest supermarket superstore, or specialty kitchen store.

scales

Accurate measuring is absolutely essential for cake making. Too much fat and the cake will sink, too much flour and the cake will be dry. A small kitchen scale can be useful. Digital add-and-weigh scales are the easiest and clearest to use as the amount is shown with pinpoint accuracy.

Unlike the more traditional balance scales, you can place your usual mixing bowl on top, press the control button to zero then add and measure out your chosen ingredients. Reset the scales to zero and you can add more ingredients to the same bowl.

Add-and-weigh scales also tend to be more compact than balance scales. The disadvantage is that the battery will run out at some point, so keep a spare handy.

If choosing spring-balanced scales make sure the small amounts are easy to read.

measuring spoons

A set of measuring spoons—from ¼ teaspoon up to 1 tablespoon—are invaluable for measuring out small quantities and ingredients such as spices, baking powder, lemon juice, vanilla extract, and oil.

When measuring out dry ingredients, all spoonfuls should be level unless otherwise stated in the recipe.

measuring cup

A glass measuring cup tends to be easier to read and longer lasting than a plastic one, providing you don't drop it on the kitchen floor! Stand it on a flat surface and bend down to read the measurement rather than hold it up to eye level.

mixing bowls

These can be of plain glass, stainless steel, china, or plastic. You will need a minimum of three in decreasing sizes, so that they fit inside each other for easy storage.

If you like to make large fruit cakes or celebration cakes, then an extra large mixing bowl may be useful as well.

cooling rack

Once baked, cakes and cookies need to be transferred to a wire rack so that the steam can escape and the bases stay dry. Choose one with narrow gaps between the wires or improvise and use the broiler rack instead.

cookie cutters

A good-quality set of plain and fluted round metal cookie cutters will last you a lifetime and can be used not only for cookies but also when making little tarts, pies, and scones.

pastry bag and tips

These are not essential but are good for piping meringues, éclairs, and cookie mixture. It's useful to have a large ½ inch fluted tip and a plain tip. Nylon pastry bags tend to be more flexible and easier to use than the thicker plastic ones.

food processor versus electric mixer

Food processors and electric mixers are both extremely useful pieces of equipment for effortlessly making creamed and rubbed-in cakes, cookies, scones, and frostings. Because a food processor has a lid there is less mess than when using an electric mixer and it can contain that inevitable fine mist of confectioners' sugar or flour.

When adding fruit, remember to swap the blade from the metal to the plastic one and to blitz for the shortest time possible so that the fruit is mixed in rather than chopped.

Both a hand-held and a free-standing electric mixer are ideal for beating, although only a hand-held electric mixer can be used for beating ingredients in a bowl over a saucepan of simmering water.

pastry brush

A pastry brush isn't essential but it is good for greasing cake pans and glazing the tops of scones.

toothpick or metal skewer

These are useful for checking whether the center of a cake is cooked.

additional useful equipment

- **Flexible plastic spatula**—perfect for folding in flour or beaten egg whites and for scooping cake mixture into cake pans.
- **Rigid spatula**—a small, 4 inch one is ideal for loosening cakes while still in their pans. A larger, 10 inch, one is good for transferring a larger cake from a cooling rack to a serving plate.
- **Rolling pin**—you probably already have one, but if buying for the first time, choose one without handles.
- **Balloon whisk**—for beating frostings and whipping cream.
- **Wooden spoon**—for mixing creamed and melted-method cakes. Choose a wooden spoon with a shorter handle for easy mixing.

preparing cake pans

Grease your cake pan by brushing on a little sunflower or vegetable oil, using a pastry brush, or by smearing a small piece of butter thinly over the inside of the pan. Even nonstick pans need a light greasing before use unless fully lined with nonstick parchment paper.

waxed paper versus nonstick parchment paper

Nonstick parchment paper, as the name suggests, is nonstick and can be used to line pans or cookie sheets without the addition of any oil or butter. Waxed paper must always be greased after shaping and pressing into a greased pan. It is usually easiest to brush it lightly with a little oil. Nonstick parchment paper is preferable when lining baking sheets for meringues, roasting pans, or deep round or square pans, where the base and side are lined.

how to line a...

Deep round cake pan Draw around the pan on nonstick parchment paper and cut out the circle. Cut a strip of paper a little taller than the pan sides and a little longer so that the paper overlaps when in the pan. Fold up a strip along the bottom edge then snip into it at intervals. Stand the paper inside the ungreased pan with the snipped edge on the base of the pan. Place the paper circle on top of this.

Deep square cake pan This technique is similar, but instead of snipping all around the bottom edge of the vertical lining paper, make cuts only where the paper will fit into the corners of the pan.

Layer pan Draw around the pan on waxed paper and cut out the circle. Press into the base of the greased pan then grease the paper.

Roasting pan or jelly roll pan Cut a rectangle of nonstick parchment paper larger than the top of the pan. Make diagonal cuts into the corners then press the paper into the base of the ungreased pan, so that the base and sides of the pan are lined and, for a jelly roll pan, the paper stands a little above the pan's sides.

Loaf pan Press a strip of waxed paper the same length as the longest side, and wide enough to cover the base and up the two long sides, into a greased pan then grease the paper. You don't need to line the short ends of the pan.

baking know-how

Cooking times are always a guide so do check on your cake's progress during cooking. Rely only on the oven's glass door if possible. Certainly, never open the door until just over halfway through cooking, when the cake will be set and at less risk of sinking. Even then, open it very slightly, just enough to see how the cake is doing. If it is cooking more quickly at the front or sides, rotate the cake so it cooks evenly.

Cakes should be an even color all over when cooked. Sponge cakes will spring back when gently pressed with fingertips. A fine skewer pushed into the middle of larger cakes should come out clean and dry.

Make sure you select the correct size pan for your cake. Pans should be measured across the base, especially if you are using a roasting pan as these normally have slightly sloping sides and a lip on the top edge.

troubleshooting

If your cake doesn't turn out as expected see if you can identify the problem from the following.

Cake cracks heavily on top
• Cake cooked at too high a temperature or on too high an oven shelf.
• Rounded rather than level teaspoons of raising agent were used.
• Too small a cake pan was used so cake is very deep.

Fruit sinks
• Too much fruit for the cake mixture too hold.
• Fruit was damp, or candied cherries, if using, were very sticky with sugar.

Cake sinks
• Oven door was opened before the cake had set.
• Cake removed from oven before it was cooked right through.
• Too much raising agent so cake rose quickly but then collapsed before mixture was set.

Cake does not rise properly
• Air was knocked out—perhaps the flour was stirred into a beaten cake rather than being gently folded in.
• Oven at too low a temperature or was accidentally turned off.
• Raising agent such as baking powder was forgotten.
• All-purpose flour used in place of self-rising flour.
• Cake cooked in too large a pan.

Cake is dry
• Not enough fat.
• Cake was overcooked.
• Not wrapped and stored in a plastic or other airtight container after baking.

storing cakes

Cakes or cookies are generally best kept in an airtight container and stored in a cool place, but store cakes with cream or cream cheese fillings or frostings in the refrigerator. Most cakes freeze well although it's best to freeze those with glacé icing or fresh fruits unfilled or uniced. For very fragile cakes open freeze until firm then wrap in plastic wrap or foil or pack into a plastic container. More robust cakes can be wrapped and then frozen. Large cakes can be sliced before freezing, and the slices interleaved with pieces of nonstick parchment paper, so that just one or two slices can be thawed as required.

Use all frozen cakes within 3 months, defrost at room temperature for 2–4 hours depending on their size. Scones and cookies are best refreshed in the oven once they are defrosted, for 5–10 minutes at 350°F.

don't forget to...

• **Use a pastry brush,** for greasing cake pans and glazing tops of scones.
• **Preheat the oven,** reducing the temperature by 18-36°F if using a fan-assisted oven.
• **Center the oven shelf,** unless you plan to cook more than one baking sheet at a time.
• **Grease and line the cake pans** before you start.
• **Use level measures.**
• **Use a timer** so that you know when to check on the cake's progress.

little cakes

pistachio & chocolate meringues

Makes **16**
Preparation time **30 minutes**
Cooking time **45–60 minutes**

3 **egg whites**
¾ cup **superfine sugar**
½ cup **shelled pistachio nuts**,
  finely chopped
5 oz **semisweet chocolate**,
  broken into pieces
⅔ cup **heavy cream**

Beat the egg whites in a large clean bowl until stiff. Gradually beat in the sugar, a teaspoonful at a time, until it has all been added. Beat for a few minutes more until the meringue mixture is thick and glossy.

Fold in the pistachios then spoon heaping teaspoonfuls of the mixture into rough swirly mounds on 2 large baking sheets lined with nonstick parchment paper.

Bake in a preheated oven, 225°F, for 45–60 minutes or until the meringues are firm and may be easily peeled off the paper. Allow to cool still on the paper.

Melt the chocolate in a heatproof bowl set over a saucepan of gently simmering water. Lift the meringues off the paper and dip the bases into the chocolate. Return to the paper, tilted on their sides and leave in a cool place until the chocolate has hardened.

To serve, whip the cream until just holding its shape then use to sandwich the meringues together in pairs. Arrange in paper bake cups, if desired, on a cake plate or stand. Eat on the day they are filled. (Left plain, the meringues will keep for 2–3 days.)

For saffron & chocolate meringues, add a large pinch of saffron threads to the egg whites when first beating them and omit the pistachios. Dip the meringues in the melted chocolate, fill with the whipped cream, and serve as above.

easter cupcakes

Makes **12**
Preparation time **20 minutes,
  plus setting**
Cooking time **15–18 minutes**

1 cup **all-purpose flour**
½ cup **superfine sugar**
½ cup **soft margarine**
1½ teaspoons **baking powder**
1½ teaspoons **vanilla extract**
2 **eggs**

For the topping
1 cup **confectioners' sugar,**
  sifted
½ teaspoon **vanilla extract**
4 teaspoons **water**
a few drops of **yellow, green,
  and pink food coloring**
jelly beans, to decorate

Put all the cupcake ingredients in a mixing bowl or a food processor and beat until smooth. Spoon the mixture into foil bake cups arranged in a greased 12-hole deep muffin pan. Bake in a preheated oven, 350°F, for 15–18 minutes until well risen and the cakes spring back when gently pressed with a fingertip. Leave to cool in the pan.

Make the topping. Mix together the confectioners' sugar, vanilla, and enough of the water to make a smooth icing. Divide the icing among 3 bowls and color each batch differently. Turn the cakes out of the pan, ice them, and decorate with jelly beans. Leave for 30 minutes for the icing to set.

For girly cupcakes, make the cupcakes as above but use just a few drops of pink food coloring to color the icing and decorate the top of each cupcake with a single pastel-colored sugared flower instead of the jelly beans.

lemon & orange drizzle cakes

Makes **12**
Preparation time **20 minutes**
Cooking time **12–15 minutes**

2 cups **self-rising flour**
1 cup **superfine sugar**
grated zest and juice of
  1 lemon
grated zest and juice of
  1 orange
3 **eggs**
2 tablespoons **milk**
½ cup **butter**, melted

Put the flour in a mixing bowl then add half the sugar and half the lemon and orange zest. Lightly beat the eggs and milk together then add to the bowl with the melted butter. Beat together until just smooth.

Spoon the mixture into the sections of a greased 12-hole deep muffin pan. Bake in a preheated oven, 375°F, for 12–15 minutes until well risen and the tops are craggy and firm to the touch.

Make the lemon and orange syrup. Put the remaining sugar and grated citrus zest in a bowl. Strain in the fruit juices then mix together until the sugar has just dissolved.

As soon as the cakes come out of the oven, loosen the edges and turn out. Arrange in a shallow dish, prick the tops with a toothpick or fork and drizzle the syrup over, little by little, until absorbed by the cakes. Allow to cool. The cakes are best served on the day they are made.

For lemon syrup cakes, make up the mixture with 2 lemons and bake as above, finishing with a lemon-only syrup. Serve warm with vanilla ice cream for a delicious dessert.

orange & raisin scones

Makes **10**
Preparation time **20 minutes**
Cooking time **10 minutes**

3 cups **self-rising flour**
¼ cup **butter**, diced
¼ cup **superfine sugar**, plus
  extra for sprinkling
½ cup **golden raisins**
grated zest of **1 orange**
1 **egg**, beaten
⅔–¾ cup **lowfat milk**

To serve
5 tablespoons **apricot jelly**
1 cup **clotted cream**

Put the flour in a mixing bowl or a food processor. Add the butter and blend with your fingertips or process until the mixture resembles fine bread crumbs. Stir in the sugar, golden raisins, and orange zest.

Add all but 1 tablespoon of the egg then gradually mix in enough of the milk to mix to a soft but not sticky dough.

Knead lightly then roll out on a lightly floured surface until ¾ inch thick. Stamp out 2¼ inch circles using a plain round cookie cutter. (Don't be tempted to roll out the dough thinner and make more scones as they will just look mean and miserly.) Transfer to a lightly greased cookie sheet. Reknead the trimmings and continue rolling and stamping out until you have made 10 scones.

Brush the tops with the reserved egg and sprinkle lightly with a little extra superfine sugar. Bake in a preheated oven, 400°F, for 10–12 minutes until well risen and the tops are golden. Allow to cool on the cookie sheet.

Serve the scones warm or just cold, split and filled with jelly and clotted cream. They are best eaten on the day they are made.

For fat rascals, make the scones as above but omit the orange zest and golden raisins and stir in ½ teaspoon ground cinnamon instead. Sprinkle the tops of the scones with 2 tablespoons superfine sugar mixed with ½ teaspoon ground cinnamon before baking as above.

maple & pecan muffins

Makes **8**
Preparation time **10 minutes**
Cooking time **20–25 minutes**

2½ cups **self-rising flour**
1 teaspoon **baking powder**
½ cup **brown sugar**
1 **egg**
3 tablespoons **maple syrup**
1 cup **milk**
¼ cup **unsalted butter**, melted
4 oz **white chocolate**, finely
  chopped
¾ cup **pecan nuts**, coarsely
  chopped

To decorate
chopped **pecans**
chopped **white chocolate**

Sift the flour and baking powder into a mixing bowl and stir in the sugar. Beat together the egg, maple syrup, milk, and melted butter and beat into the dry ingredients until mixed. Fold in the chocolate and pecan nuts.

Divide the mixture evenly among 8 paper bake cups arranged in a 12-hole deep muffin pan and top with some extra chopped nuts and chocolate. Bake in a preheated oven, 400°F, for 20–25 minutes until risen and golden. Transfer to a cooling rack to cool.

For milk chocolate & walnut muffins, make the muffins as above but replace the white chocolate with 4 oz finely chopped milk chocolate and the pecan nuts with ½ cup coarsely chopped walnuts.

fruited griddle cakes

Makes **30**
Preparation time **25 minutes**
Cooking time **18 minutes**

2 cups **self-rising flour**
½ cup **butter**, diced
½ cup **superfine sugar**, plus
   extra for sprinkling
⅛ cup **currants**
⅛ cup **golden raisins**
1 teaspoon **ground mixed
   spice**
grated zest of ½ **lemon**
1 **egg**, beaten
1 tablespoon **milk**, if needed
oil, for greasing

Put the flour in a mixing bowl or a food processor. Add the butter and blend with your fingertips or process until the mixture resembles fine bread crumbs. Stir in the sugar, dried fruit, spice, and lemon zest.

Add the egg then gradually mix in milk, if needed, to make a smooth dough. Knead lightly then roll out on a lightly floured surface until ¼ inch thick. Stamp out 2 inch circles using a fluted round cookie cutter. Reknead the trimmings and continue rolling and stamping out until all the dough has been used.

Pour a little oil onto a piece of folded paper towel and use to grease a griddle or heavy nonstick skillet. Heat the pan then add the cakes in batches, regreasing the griddle or pan as needed, and fry over a medium to low heat for about 3 minutes each side until golden brown and cooked through. Serve warm, sprinkled with a little extra sugar or spread with butter, if desired. Store in an airtight container for up to 2 days.

For orange & cinnamon griddle cakes, use the grated zest of ½ orange instead of the lemon, and 1 teaspoon ground cinnamon in place of the mixed spice. Continue the recipe as above.

hot cross buns

Makes **12**

Preparation time **1 hour,
plus standing and rising**

Cooking time **20 minutes**

2 tablespoons **active dry
yeast**

1 teaspoon **sugar**

⅔ cup **milk**, warmed

4 tablespoons warm **water**

4 cups **bread flour**

1 teaspoon **salt**

½ teaspoon **ground mixed
spice**

½ teaspoon **ground cinnamon**

½ teaspoon **grated nutmeg**

¼ cup **superfine sugar**

¼ cup **butter**, melted and
cooled

1 **egg**, beaten

¾ cup **currants**

¼ cup **chopped candied peel**

3 oz **ready-made shortcrust
pastry**

For the glaze

3 tablespoons **superfine
sugar**

4 tablespoons **milk and water**

Blend the yeast and sugar into the warmed milk and water. Stir into 1 cup of the flour and leave in a warm place for about 20 minutes. Sift the remaining flour into a bowl, add the salt, spices, and superfine sugar.

Add the butter and egg to the yeast mixture. Stir this into the flour and mix well. Add the dried fruit and mix to a fairly soft dough. Add a little water if necessary.

Turn out the dough onto a lightly floured surface and knead well. Place in an oiled plastic bag and allow to rise for 1–1½ hours at room temperature until doubled in size. Turn out onto a floured surface and knead with your knuckles to knock out the air bubbles.

Divide the dough and shape into 12 round buns. Flatten each slightly then space well apart on floured cookie sheets. Cover and put in a warm place again to rise for 20–30 minutes until doubled in size. Meanwhile, thinly roll out the pastry and cut it into 24 thin strips about 3½ inches long.

Dampen the strips and lay 2, damp side down, in a cross over each bun. Bake in a preheated oven, 375°F, for 20 minutes or until golden brown and firm.

Make the glaze. Dissolve the sugar in the milk and water mixture over a low heat. Brush the cooked buns twice with the glaze, then serve hot, split, and buttered.

For gingered fruit buns, use ¾ cup luxury dried fruit instead of the currants, and 2 tablespoons chopped crystallized ginger in place of the candied peel. Omit the pastry crosses and glaze as above.

churros

Makes **12**
Preparation time **20 minutes**
Cooking time **6–9 minutes**

1¾ cups **all-purpose flour**
¼ teaspoon **salt**
5 tablespoons **superfine
  sugar**
1¼ cups **water**
1 **egg**, beaten
1 **egg yolk**
1 teaspoon **vanilla extract**
4 cups **sunflower oil**
1 teaspoon **ground cinnamon**

Mix the flour, salt, and 1 tablespoon of the sugar in
a bowl. Pour the water into a saucepan and bring to a
boil. Take off the heat, add the flour mixture, and beat
well. Then return to the heat and stir until it forms
a smooth ball that leaves the sides of the pan almost
clean. Remove from the heat and allow to cool for
10 minutes.

Gradually beat the whole egg, egg yolk, then the
vanilla into the flour mixture until smooth. Spoon into a
large nylon pastry bag fitted with a ½ inch wide plain tip.

Pour the oil into a medium saucepan to a depth of
1 inch. Heat to 340°F on a candy thermometer or
pipe a tiny amount of the mixture into the oil. If the
oil bubbles instantly it is ready to use. Pipe coils,
S-shapes and squiggly lines into the oil, in small
batches, cutting the ends off with kitchen scissors.
Cook the churros for 2–3 minutes until they float and
are golden, turning over if needed to brown evenly.

Lift the churros out of the oil, drain well on paper
towels, then sprinkle with the remaining sugar mixed
with the cinnamon. Continue piping and frying until
all the mixture has been used. Serve warm or cold.
They are best eaten on the day they are made.

For orange churros, add the grated zest of 1 orange
and omit the vanilla extract. Continue as above.
Sprinkle with plain superfine sugar when cooked.

snow-covered ginger muffins

Makes **12**
Preparation time **30 minutes,**
  plus setting
Cooking time **10–15 minutes**

½ cup **butter**
½ cup **maple syrup**
½ cup **light brown sugar**
2 cups **self-rising flour**
1 teaspoon **baking powder**
1 teaspoon **ground ginger**
2 **eggs**
½ cup **milk**
3 tablespoons chopped
  crystallized ginger, plus
  extra to decorate

For the icing
1¾ cups **confectioners' sugar**
5–6 teaspoons **water**
2 pieces **crystallized ginger,**
  sliced

Put the butter, syrup, and sugar in a saucepan and
heat gently, stirring until the butter has melted. Mix
the flour, baking powder, and ground ginger in a bowl.
Beat the eggs and milk in another bowl.

Remove the butter saucepan from the heat, then beat
in the flour mixture. Gradually beat in the egg and milk
mixture, then stir in the chopped crystallized ginger.

Divide the mixture evenly among paper bake cups
arranged in a 12-hole deep muffin pan and bake in a
preheated oven, 350°F, for 10–15 minutes until well
risen and cracked. Allow to cool in the pan.

Make the icing. Sift the confectioners' sugar into
a bowl and gradually mix in the water to create a
smooth spoonable icing. Drizzle random lines of icing
from a spoon over the muffins and complete with
slices of crystallized ginger. Allow the icing to harden
for 30 minutes before serving.

For cinnamon & orange muffins, replace the
ground ginger with 1 teaspoon ground cinnamon
and use the grated zest of ½ orange instead of the
crystallized ginger. In the icing, replace the water
with 4–5 teaspoons orange juice and decorate with
a little extra grated orange zest.

viennese whirls

Makes **8**
Preparation time **20 minutes**
Cooking time **15 minutes**

½ cup **butter**, at room
 temperature
½ cup **confectioners' sugar**
2 **egg yolks**
½ teaspoon **vanilla extract**
1 cup **self-rising flour**
3 tablespoons **cornstarch**
10 frozen **raspberries**
1 tablespoon **strawberry or
 seedless raspberry jelly**
sifted **confectioners' sugar**,
 for dusting

Beat the butter and sugar together in a mixing bowl until pale and creamy. Gradually beat in the egg yolks and the vanilla then gradually beat in the flour and cornstarch until smooth.

Spoon the mixture into a large nylon pastry bag fitted with a large star tip. Pipe double thickness circles of the mixture into 8 paper bake cups arranged in a 12-hole shallow muffin pan. Press a still frozen raspberry in the center of each.

Bake in a preheated oven, 350°F, for about 15 minutes until pale golden. Allow to cool in the pan then add tiny spoonfuls of jelly to the center of each cake and dust lightly with sifted confectioners' sugar. Transfer to a serving plate. These are best eaten on the day they are made.

For jumblies, pipe S-shapes of the above mixture on to greased cookie sheets. Decorate with sugar sprinkles and bake as above for 6–8 minutes until pale golden.

blueberry & lemon muffins

Makes **12**
Preparation time **15 minutes**
Cooking time **18–20 minutes**

1 cup **malthouse, granary** or
  whole-wheat flour
1 cup **all-purpose flour**
3 teaspoons **baking powder**
½ cup **light brown sugar**
1⅓ cups **blueberries**
grated zest and juice of
  1 lemon
4 tablespoons **olive or
  sunflower oil**
¼ cup **margarine or butter**,
  melted
3 **eggs**, beaten
⅔ cup **lowfat milk**

For the lemon frosting
1 cup **confectioners' sugar**
juice of ½ **lemon**

Mix the flours, baking powder, sugar, and blueberries together in a mixing bowl. Put the remaining ingredients in a pitcher and fork together. Add to the dry ingredients and mix briefly with a fork.

Divide the mixture evenly among paper bake cups arranged in a 12-hole deep muffin pan. Bake in a preheated oven, 375°F, for 18–20 minutes until well risen and the tops are cracked. Allow to cool in the tin for 15 minutes.

Make the frosting. Sift the confectioners' sugar into a bowl and gradually mix in enough lemon juice to make a thin spoonable icing. Take the muffins out of the pan and drizzle frosting from a spoon in random lines over the top. Allow to harden slightly and serve the muffins while still warm.

For raspberry & white chocolate muffins,
replace the blueberries with the same quantity of fresh raspberries. Bake as above then drizzle with 4 oz melted white chocolate instead of the lemon frosting, sprinkling with a little grated white chocolate, if desired.

mini cappuccino cakes

Makes **12**
Preparation time **30 minutes**
Cooking time **12–14 minutes**

3 teaspoons **instant coffee**
2 teaspoons **boiling water**
¾ cup **soft margarine**
¾ cup **light brown sugar**
1½ cups **self-rising flour**
½ teaspoon **baking powder**
3 **eggs**

To decorate
1¼ cups **heavy cream**
3 oz **semisweet or white chocolate curls**

Dissolve the coffee in the boiling water.

Beat the remaining cake ingredients in a mixing bowl or a food processor until smooth. Stir in the dissolved coffee. Divide the mixture evenly among the greased and base-lined sections of a 12-hole deep muffin pan and spread the surfaces level.

Bake in a preheated oven, 350°F, for 12–14 minutes until well risen and the cakes spring back when gently pressed with a fingertip. Allow to cool in the pan for 5 minutes then loosen the edges, turn out onto a cooling rack and peel off the lining paper. Allow to cool completely.

Turn each cake the right way up then slice in half horizontally. Whip the cream until softly peaking then use to sandwich the cakes together in pairs and spread the remainder on the tops. Sprinkle with the chocolate curls. These are best eaten on the day they are made.

For mini victoria sandwich cakes, omit the dissolved coffee and add 1 teaspoon vanilla extract to the cake mixture. Fill the baked cakes with a layer of strawberry jelly and ⅔ cup whipped heavy cream. Dust the tops with sifted confectioners' sugar.

lamingtons

Makes **24**
Preparation time **20 minutes,
 plus overnight standing**
Cooking time **25–30 minutes**

½ cup **unsalted butter**, at
 room temperature
½ cup **superfine sugar**
2 **eggs**, lightly beaten
2 cups **self-rising flour**
pinch of **salt**
4 tablespoons **milk**
1 teaspoon **vanilla extract**

For the icing
3½ cups **confectioners'
 sugar**
1 cup **cocoa powder**
about ⅔ cup **boiling water**
2½ cups **shredded coconut**

Beat the butter and sugar together in a mixing bowl until pale and creamy. Beat in the eggs, a little at a time, until incorporated. Sift in the flour and salt and fold into the creamed mixture with the milk and vanilla. Alternatively, beat all the cake ingredients together in a food processor until smooth.

Transfer the mixture to a greased and base-lined 7 x 10 inch cake pan. Spread the surface level with a spatula and bake in a preheated oven, 375°F, for 25–30 minutes until risen and firm to the touch. Allow the cake to cool in the pan for 5 minutes then loosen the edges, turn out onto a cooling rack and peel off the lining paper. Leave out overnight.

Make the icing. Sift the confectioners' sugar and cocoa powder into a bowl, make a well in the center and beat in the boiling water to make a smooth chocolate icing with a pouring consistency.

Cut the cooled cake into 24 pieces. Use 2 forks to dip each cake into the icing and then immediately coat with the coconut all over. Allow to set on parchment paper.

For raspberry splits, when the cake is cool, cut it in half and sandwich back together with 6 tablespoons raspberry jelly. Sift 1¾ cups confectioners' sugar into a bowl and mix in 5–6 teaspoons cold water to make a spreadable icing. Spread over the cake and decorate with sugar sprinkles. Allow to harden for 30 minutes, then cut into 24 squares.

chunky chocolate muffins

Makes **12**
Preparation time **20 minutes**
Cooking time **15–18 minutes**

2¼ cups **all-purpose flour**
¼ cup **cocoa powder**
3 teaspoons **baking powder**
⅔ cup **superfine sugar**
⅓ cup **butter**, melted
3 **eggs**, beaten
⅔ cup **milk**
1 teaspoon **vanilla extract**
7 oz **white chocolate**, finely
   chopped
4 oz **semisweet or milk
   chocolate**, broken into
   pieces

Sift the flour, cocoa powder, and baking powder into a mixing bowl. Add the sugar and stir together.

Add the melted butter, beaten eggs, milk, and vanilla and fork together until almost mixed. Stir in the chopped white chocolate.

Spoon into paper bake cups arranged in a 12-hole deep muffin pan and bake in a preheated oven, 400°F, for 18–20 minutes until well risen. Allow to cool in the tin for 5 minutes then transfer to a cooling rack.

Melt the semisweet or milk chocolate in a heatproof bowl set over a saucepan of gently simmering water, then drizzle the chocolate in random lines over the top of each muffin.

Serve the muffins warm or cold. They are best eaten on the day they are made.

For white chocolate & cranberry muffins, soak ⅓ cup dried cranberries in 2 tablespoons boiling water for 10 minutes. Use 2½ cups all-purpose flour instead of the mix of flour and cocoa powder. Continue the recipe above, adding the drained soaked cranberries along with the chopped white chocolate. Omit the melted chocolate topping and dust with a little sifted confectioners' sugar to serve.

banana & raisin drop scones

Makes **10**
Preparation time **10 minutes**
Cooking time **8 minutes**

1 cup **self-rising flour**
2 tablespoons **superfine
  sugar**
½ teaspoon **baking powder**
1 small ripe **banana**, about
  4 oz with skin on, peeled
  and roughly mashed
1 **egg**, beaten
⅔ cup **milk**
¼ cup **golden raisins**
oil, for greasing
**butter, honey, corn or maple
  syrup**, to serve

Put the flour, sugar, and baking powder in a mixing
bowl. Add the mashed banana with the egg. Gradually
beat in the milk with a fork until the mixture resembles
a smooth thick batter. Stir in the golden raisins.

Pour a little oil onto a piece of folded paper towel
and use to grease a griddle or heavy nonstick skillet.
Heat the pan then drop heaping dessertspoonfuls of
the mixture, well spaced apart, onto the pan. Cook
for 2 minutes until bubbles appear on the top and
the undersides are golden. Turn over and cook for
1–2 minutes more until the second side is done.

Serve warm, topped with butter, honey, corn or maple
syrup. These are best eaten on the day they are made.

For summer berry drop scones, make the above
recipe in the same way but stir in ⅔ cup mixed
fresh blueberries and raspberries instead of the
golden raisins.

spiced pear & cranberry muffins

Makes **12**
Preparation time **20 minutes**
Cooking time **15–18 minutes**

⅓ cup **dried cranberries**
2 tablespoons **boiling water**
3 small ripe **pears**
2½ cups **all-purpose flour**
3 teaspoons **baking powder**
1 teaspoon **ground cinnamon**
½ teaspoon **grated nutmeg**
½ cup **superfine sugar**, plus
   extra for sprinkling
¼ cup **butter**, melted
3 tablespoons **olive oil**
3 **eggs**
⅔ cup **low-fat plain yogurt**

Put the cranberries in a cup, add the boiling water and allow to soak for 10 minutes. Meanwhile, quarter, core, peel, and dice the pears.

Place the flour, baking powder, spices, and sugar in a mixing bowl. Fork the melted butter, oil, eggs, and yogurt together in another bowl then combine with the flour mixture.

Drain the cranberries, add to the flour mixture with the pears and mix briefly, then spoon into paper muffin cups arranged in a 12-hole deep muffin pan and sprinkle with a little extra superfine sugar.

Bake in a preheated oven, 400°F, for 15–18 minutes until well risen and golden. Allow to cool in the tin for 5 minutes then transfer to a cooling rack. Serve warm or cold. They are best eaten on the day they are made.

For blueberry & cranberry muffins, omit the pear and spices from the recipe above and add 1 cup fresh blueberries and the grated zest of 1 lemon instead, stirring them into the flour mixture at the same time as the soaked cranberries. Continue the recipe as above.

strawberry & lavender shortcakes

Makes **8**
Preparation time **30 minutes**
Cooking time **10–12 minutes**

1¼ cups **all-purpose flour**
2 tablespoons **ground rice**
½ cup **butter**, diced
¼ cup **superfine sugar**
1 tablespoon **lavender petals**

To decorate
1⅔ cups **strawberries** (or a
    mixture of strawberries and
    raspberries)
⅔ cup **heavy cream**
16 small **lavender flowers**
    (optional)
sifted **confectioners' sugar**,
    for dusting

Put the flour and ground rice in a mixing bowl or a
food processor. Add the butter and blend with your
fingertips or process until the mixture resembles fine
bread crumbs.

Stir in the sugar and lavender petals and squeeze the
crumbs together with your hands to form a smooth
ball. Knead lightly then roll out on a lightly floured
surface until ¼ inch thick. Stamp out 3 inch circles
using a fluted round cookie cutter. Transfer to an
ungreased cookie sheet. Reknead the trimmings and
continue rolling and stamping out until you have made
16 cookies.

Prick with a fork, bake in a preheated oven, 325°F, for
10–12 minutes until pale golden. Allow to cool on the
cookie sheet.

To serve, halve 4 of the smallest strawberries, hull
and slice the rest. Whip the cream and spoon over
8 of the cookies. Top with the sliced strawberries
then the remaining cookies. Spoon the remaining
cream on top and decorate with the reserved halved
strawberries and tiny sprigs of lavender, if desired.
Dust lightly with sifted confectioners' sugar. These
are best eaten on the day they are filled, but the
plain cookies can be stored in an airtight container
for up to 3 days.

For lemon & blueberry shortcakes, follow the
recipe above but add the grated zest of 1 lemon to
the cookie dough instead of the lavender petals. Fill
with whipped cream and 1¾ cups fresh blueberries.

apricot & sunflower muffins

Makes **12**
Preparation time **20 minutes**
Cooking time **15–18 minutes**

1¾ cups **self-rising whole-wheat flour**
1 teaspoon **baking powder**
⅔ cup **light brown sugar**
grated zest of **1 orange**
3 **eggs**
¾ cup **sour cream**
7½ oz can **apricot halves in natural juice**, drained and roughly chopped, the juice reserved
3 tablespoons **sunflower seeds**

Stir the flour, baking powder, sugar, and orange zest together in a mixing bowl.

Beat the eggs in a smaller bowl then mix in the sour cream. Add to the flour mixture with the chopped apricots and fork together until just mixed, adding 2–3 tablespoons of the reserved canned apricot juice to make a soft spoonable consistency.

Spoon the mixture into paper muffin cups arranged in a 12-hole deep muffin pan and sprinkle with the sunflower seeds. Bake in a preheated oven, 400°F, for 15–18 minutes until well risen and the tops are cracked. Allow to cool in the pan for 5 minutes then transfer to a cooling rack. Serve warm or cold. These are best eaten on the day they are made.

For peach & orange muffins, add the diced flesh from 1 large peach, the grated zest of 1 orange and 2–3 tablespoons orange juice to the basic muffin mixture above instead of the canned apricots and their juice. Continue the recipe as above.

banoffee meringues

Makes **8**
Preparation time **30 minutes**
Cooking time **1–1¼ hours**

3 **egg whites**
½ cup **light brown sugar**
⅓ cup **superfine sugar**

To decorate
1 small ripe **banana**
1 tablespoon **lemon juice**
⅔ cup **heavy cream**
8 tablespoons ready-made
   fudge ice cream sauce

Beat the egg whites in a large clean bowl until stiff. Gradually beat in the sugars, a teaspoonful at a time, until it has all been added. Beat for a few minutes more until the meringue mixture is thick and glossy.

Using a dessertspoon, take a large scoop of meringue mixture then scoop off the first spoon using a second spoon and drop onto a large baking sheet lined with nonstick parchment paper to make an oval-shaped meringue. Continue until all the mixture has been used.

Bake in a preheated oven, 225°F, for 1–1¼ hours or until the meringues are firm and may be easily peeled off the paper. Allow to cool still on the paper.

To serve, roughly mash the banana with the lemon juice. Whip the cream until it forms soft swirls then beat in 2 tablespoons of the fudge sauce. Combine with the mashed banana then use to sandwich the meringues together in pairs and arrange in paper bake cups. Drizzle with the remaining fudge sauce and serve immediately. Unfilled meringues may be stored in an airtight container for up to 3 days.

For coffee toffee meringues, make the meringues as above. To make the filling, whip the cream, then stir in 1–2 teaspoons instant coffee, dissolved in 1 teaspoon boiling water. Use to sandwich the meringues together in pairs. Drizzle fudge sauce over the top of the meringues.

hazelnut & blueberry cakes

Makes **12**
Preparation time **20 minutes**
Cooking time **20 minutes**

3 **eggs**
⅔ cup **reduced-fat sour
    cream**
⅔ cup **superfine sugar**
½ cup **finely ground
    hazelnuts**
1½ cups **all-purpose flour**
1½ teaspoons **baking powder**
1 cup **fresh blueberries**
2 tablespoons **hazelnuts**,
    roughly chopped
sifted **confectioners' sugar**,
    for dusting

Put the eggs, sour cream, and sugar in a mixing bowl and beat together until smooth. Add the ground hazelnuts, flour, and baking powder and mix together.

Spoon the mixture into paper bake cups arranged in a 12-hole deep muffin pan and divide the blueberries evenly among them, pressing lightly into the mixture. Sprinkle with chopped hazelnuts.

Bake in a preheated oven, 350°F, for about 20 minutes until well risen and golden. Dust the tops with a little sifted confectioners' sugar and allow to cool in the pan. These are best eaten on the day they are made.

For almond & raspberry cakes, follow the recipe above but use ½ cup ground almonds in place of the ground hazelnuts and use the same quantity of raspberries instead of the blueberries. Sprinkle the tops of the cakes with 2 tablespoons slivered almonds and bake as above.

tangy lemon cupcakes

Makes **12**
Preparation time **25 minutes**
Cooking time **15–18 minutes**

½ cup **soft margarine**
½ cup **superfine sugar**
2 **eggs**, beaten
1 cup **self-rising flour**
grated zest and juice of
　1 **lemon**
1½ cups **confectioners'**
　sugar, sifted
yellow or pink food coloring
sugar flowers, to decorate

Beat the margarine, sugar, eggs, flour, and lemon zest in a mixing bowl or a food processor until smooth.

Divide the mixture evenly among foil bake cups arranged in a 12-hole deep muffin pan and spread the surfaces level. Bake in a preheated oven, 350°F, for 15–18 minutes until golden and the cakes spring back when gently pressed with a fingertip. Allow to cool in the pan.

Mix the confectioners' sugar with 4–5 teaspoons of the lemon juice to make a smooth thick spreadable paste. Trim the tops of the cakes level if needed. Spoon half the icing over half the cakes and ease into a smooth layer with a wetted round-bladed knife.

Color the remaining icing pale yellow or pink and spoon it over the remaining cakes. Decorate with homemade pastel-colored flowers stamped out from ready-to-use icing or use store-bought sugar flowers. Allow to harden for 30 minutes. Store in an airtight container for up to 3 days.

For candy cupcakes, add 1 teaspoon vanilla extract to the cake mixture instead of the lemon zest. Add 6–7 teaspoons water instead of lemon juice to the confectioners' sugar and mix until smooth. Color half pale pink and half blue. Spoon over the cakes and decorate with tiny candies instead of sugar flowers.

whole-wheat molasses scones

Makes **14**

Preparation time **15 minutes**

Cooking time **6–8 minutes**

3 cups **malted bread flour**,
  plus extra for sprinkling
  (optional)

¼ cup **butter**, diced

¼ cup **light brown sugar**

3 teaspoons **baking powder**

1 teaspoon **baking soda**

8 tablespoons **low-fat plain
  yogurt**

2 tablespoons **molasses**

1 **egg**, beaten

To serve

2 cups **sour cream**

1½ cups **strawberry jam**

Put the flour in a mixing bowl or a food processor. Add the butter and blend with your fingertips or process until the mixture resembles fine bread crumbs. Stir in the sugar and baking powder.

Stir the baking soda into the yogurt then add to the flour mixture with the molasses. Gradually mix in enough of the beaten egg to form a soft but not sticky dough. Knead lightly then roll out on a lightly floured surface until ¾ inch thick.

Working quickly, cut out 2¼ inch circles using a plain cookie cutter. Transfer to a greased baking sheet. Reknead the trimmings and continue rolling and stamping out until all the mixture has been used. Add to the baking sheet and sprinkle the tops with a little extra flour or leave plain if preferred.

Bake in a preheated oven, 425°F, for 6–8 minutes until well risen and browned. Transfer the scones to a napkin-lined basket and serve warm or cold, split and topped with sour cream and jam. They are best eaten on the day they are made.

For date & walnut scones, follow the basic recipe above but stir ½ cup ready-chopped dried dates and ¼ cup chopped walnut pieces into the scone mix just after adding the molasses. Continue the recipe as above.

mocha cupcakes

Makes **12**
Preparation time **15 minutes,
plus cooling**
Cooking time **20 minutes**

1 cup **water**
1 cup **superfine sugar**
½ cup **unsalted butter**
2 tablespoons **cocoa powder**,
sifted
½ teaspoon **baking soda**
2 tablespoons **instant coffee**
2 cups **self-rising flour**
2 **eggs**, lightly beaten
12 **chocolate-coated coffee
beans**, to decorate

For the frosting
5 oz **semisweet chocolate**,
broken into pieces
⅔ cup **unsalted butter**, diced
2 tablespoons **corn syrup**

Put the water and sugar in a saucepan and heat
gently, stirring, until the sugar has dissolved. Stir in the
butter, cocoa powder, baking soda, and instant coffee
and bring to a boil. Simmer for 5 minutes, remove from
the heat and set aside to cool.

Beat the flour and eggs into the cooled coffee and
chocolate mixture until smooth. Divide the mixture
evenly among foil bake cups arranged in a 12-hole
deep muffin pan. Bake in a preheated oven, 350°F, for
20 minutes until risen and firm. Transfer to a cooling
rack to cool.

Make the frosting. Put the chocolate, butter, and syrup
in a heatproof bowl set over a saucepan of gently
simmering water, stirring until melted. Remove from
the heat and allow to cool to room temperature, then
chill until thickened. Spread over the cupcakes, top
with a chocolate coffee bean and allow to set.

For double chocolate cupcakes, omit the instant
coffee from the cake mix and decorate the frosting
with some white chocolate curls instead of the
chocolate-covered beans.

raspberry & coconut friands

Makes **9**
Preparation time **10 minutes**
Cooking time **18–20 minutes**

¾ cup **all-purpose flour**
1 cup **confectioners' sugar**
1 cup **ground almonds**
⅔ cup **shredded coconut**
grated zest of **1 lemon**
5 **egg whites**
⅔ cup **unsalted butter**, melted
1 cup **raspberries**

Sift the flour and confectioners' sugar into a mixing bowl and stir in the ground almonds, coconut, and lemon zest.

Beat the egg whites in a large clean bowl until frothy then fold into the dry ingredients. Add the melted butter and stir until evenly combined.

Spoon the mixture into 9 lightly oiled friand pans (or a shallow muffin pan). Top each friand with a few raspberries and bake in a preheated oven, 400°F, for 18–20 minutes until a toothpick inserted into the center comes out clean. Allow to cool in the pans for 5 minutes then turn out onto a cooling rack to cool completely.

For apricot & pistachio friands, replace the shredded coconut with ⅓ cup shelled and chopped pistachios and replace the raspberries with the same quantity of diced fresh apricots. Continue the recipe as above.

cookies

fairings

Makes **12**
Preparation time **15 minutes**
Cooking time **16–20 minutes**

¾ cup **all-purpose flour**
1 teaspoon **baking powder**
½ teaspoon **baking soda**
½ teaspoon **ground cinnamon**
½ teaspoon **ground ginger**
¼ teaspoon **ground allspice** or
   mixed spice
finely grated zest of 1 **lemon**
¼ cup **butter**, diced
¼ cup **superfine sugar**
2 tablespoons **corn syrup**

Mix the flour, baking powder, baking soda, spices, and lemon zest together in a mixing bowl. Add the butter and blend with your fingertips until the mixture resembles fine bread crumbs.

Stir in the sugar, add the syrup, then mix together first with a spoon then squeeze the crumbs together with your hands to form a ball.

Shape the dough into a log then slice into 12. Roll each piece into a ball and arrange on 2 large greased cookie sheets, leaving space between for them to spread during cooking.

Cook one baking sheet at a time in the center of a preheated oven, 350°F, for 8–10 minutes or until the cookie tops are cracked and golden.

Allow to harden for 1–2 minutes then loosen and transfer to a cooling rack to cool completely. Store in an airtight container for up to 3 days.

For chocolate ginger yo-yo's, follow the recipe above but use 1 teaspoon ground ginger instead of the 3 spices and the grated zest of ½ small orange instead of 1 lemon. Shape into 20 smaller cookies, bake for 5–6 minutes as above, then transfer to a cooling rack to cool completely. Melt 3 oz semisweet chocolate, then use a little to sandwich cookies together in pairs. Drizzle the rest over the top of the cookies. Serve when the chocolate has hardened.

easter cookies

Makes **18**
Preparation time **20 minutes**
Cooking time **10 minutes**

2 cups **all-purpose flour**
⅓ cup **cornstarch**
¾ cup **butter**, diced
½ cup **superfine sugar**
a few drops of **vanilla extract**

To decorate
1 **egg white**
2¼ cups **confectioners'
  sugar**, sifted
1 teaspoon **lemon juice**
selection of **liquid or paste
  food colorings**

Put the flour and cornstarch in a mixing bowl or a
food processor. Add the butter and blend with your
fingertips or process until the mixture resembles fine
bread crumbs. Stir in the sugar and vanilla until mixed,
then squeeze the crumbs together with your hands to
form a smooth ball.

Knead lightly then roll out thinly on a lightly floured
surface. Stamp out festive shapes using cookie cutters
and transfer to ungreased cookie sheets. Reknead the
trimmings and continue rolling and stamping out until all
the dough has been used.

Prick the shapes with a fork, then bake in a preheated
oven, 350°F, for 10 minutes or until pale golden. Allow
to cool on the cookie sheet.

Make the icing. Place the egg white in a bowl. Gradually
mix in the confectioners' sugar and lemon juice to give a
smooth consistency. Add extra water if the icing seems
too thick. Divide between bowls and color as you desire.

Spoon the icing into waxed paper pastry bags, snip
off the tips and pipe outlines around the edge of the
cookies. Allow to harden for 10 minutes. Fill in the rest
of the surface of the cookie with the same color icing to
create a smooth evenly covered cookie top. Allow to dry.
Finally, pipe white icing over the top of the colored
surface to outline and make specific features.

For numberelli cookies, follow the recipe above,
then roll out the cookie dough and stamp out large
numbers with specialist cutters. Bake and ice with
brightly colored icing, decorating with sugar strands.

chocolate florentines

Makes **26**
Preparation time **30 minutes**
Cooking time **15–20 minutes**

½ cup **butter**

½ cup **superfine sugar**

⅓ cup **multicolored candied
cherries**, roughly chopped

¾ cup **slivered almonds**

2 oz **whole candied peel**,
finely chopped

½ cup **hazelnuts**, roughly
chopped

2 tablespoons **all-purpose
flour**

5 oz **semisweet dark
chocolate**, broken into
pieces

Put the butter and sugar in a saucepan and heat
gently until the butter has melted and the sugar
dissolved. Remove the pan from the heat and stir in
all the remaining ingredients except the chocolate.

Spoon tablespoons of the mixture, well spaced apart,
onto 3 baking sheets lined with nonstick parchment
paper. Flatten the mounds slightly. Cook one baking
sheet at a time in the center of a preheated oven,
350°F, for 5–7 minutes until the nuts are golden.

After removing each baking sheet from the oven,
neaten and shape the edges of the cooked cookies by
placing a slightly larger plain round cookie cutter over
the top and rotating to smooth and tidy up the edges.
Allow to cool.

Melt the chocolate in a heatproof bowl set over a
saucepan of gently simmering water. Peel the cookies
off the lining paper and arrange upside down on a
cooling rack. Spoon the melted chocolate over the
flat underside of the cookies and spread the surfaces
level. Allow to cool and harden.

For white chocolate & ginger florentines, add
2 tablespoons ready-chopped crystallized ginger to
the candied fruit and nut mixture. Spread the cooked
cookies with melted white chocolate instead of
semisweet chocolate as above.

ginger snowmen

Makes **12**
Preparation time **30 minutes**
Cooking time **7–8 minutes**

1 ¼ cups **all-purpose flour**
¼ cup **superfine sugar**
1 teaspoon **ground ginger**
½ cup **butter**, diced
24 small **silver balls or
 tiny candies**
2 oz **ready-to-use pink icing**
2 oz **ready-to-use blue icing**
small tube **black decorator
 frosting**

For the icing
1 cup **confectioners' sugar**
pinch of **ground ginger**
5 teaspoons **water**

Put the flour, sugar, and ground ginger in a mixing bowl or a food processor. Add the butter and blend with your fingertips or process until the mixture resembles fine bread crumbs.

Continue mixing, or squeeze the crumbs together with your hands to form a soft ball. Knead lightly, then roll out thinly between 2 pieces of nonstick parchment paper.

Cut out snowmen shapes using a 4 inch cookie cutter then transfer to ungreased cookie sheets. Bake in a preheated oven, 350°F, for 7–8 minutes until pale golden. Allow to cool on the cookie sheets then transfer to a cooling rack.

Make the icing. Sift the confectioners' sugar and ground ginger into a bowl. Gradually mix in the water to make a smooth thin icing. Spoon over the cookies and allow to drizzle over the edges. Add the silver balls or tiny candies for eyes, then allow to dry and harden.

Decorate the snowmen with scarves, hats, and pompoms made from the ready-to-use icing, sticking the pompoms with a little water. Pipe on small, black, smiling mouths. Allow to harden for 1 hour, before serving.

For halloween pumpkins, replace the ginger in the mix with 1 teaspoon ground cinnamon. Stamp out 3 inch circles using a plain round cookie cutter and bake as above. Make up the icing using 1 ½ cups confectioners' sugar and 6–7 teaspoons fresh orange juice and color orange with a little food coloring. Spoon over the cookies and leave until almost set. Use yellow, black, and green ready-to-use icing to decorate the faces.

coffee kisses

Makes **10**

Preparation time **25 minutes, plus chilling**

Cooking time **8–10 minutes**

2 teaspoons **instant coffee**

1 teaspoon **boiling water**

⅓ cup **butter**, at room temperature

¼ cup **light brown sugar**

1 cup **self-rising flour**

For the filling

2 teaspoons **instant coffee**

2 teaspoons **boiling water**

¼ cup **butter**, at room temperature

1 cup **confectioners' sugar**, sifted

Dissolve the coffee in the boiling water. Beat the butter and sugar together in a mixing bowl until pale and creamy. Add the dissolved coffee then gradually mix in the flour to make a smooth soft dough.

Shape the dough into a log then chill for 15 minutes. Slice the chilled log into 20 pieces. Roll each piece into a ball, arrange on 2 greased cookie sheets and flatten slightly by pressing with a fork. Bake in a preheated oven, 350°F, for 8–10 minutes until browned. Allow the cookies to cool for 5 minutes then transfer to a cooling rack to cool completely.

Make the filling. Dissolve the coffee in the boiling water. Beat the butter and confectioners' sugar together then stir in the dissolved coffee until smooth and fluffy. Use to sandwich the biscuits together in pairs. Eat within 2 days.

For chocolate kisses, omit the dissolved coffee from the cookie dough and substitute 2 tablespoons cocoa powder for the same quantity of flour. Shape as above, then use 2 oz milk chocolate, melted, in the filling in place of the dissolved coffee.

74

maple cookies

Makes **40**
Preparation time **20 minutes,**
 plus setting
Cooking time **12–15 minutes**

6 tablespoons **maple syrup**
¼ cup **superfine sugar**
1 teaspoon **baking soda**
1 **egg yolk**
½ cup **butter**, melted
1¼ cups **all-purpose flour**
¼ teaspoon **ground cinnamon**
3 oz **semisweet chocolate**,
 broken into pieces
3 oz **white chocolate**, broken
 into pieces

Stir the maple syrup, sugar, baking soda, and egg yolk into the melted butter then mix in the flour and cinnamon. Beat to a smooth creamy dough.

Drop teaspoons of the mixture, spaced slightly apart, onto baking sheets lined with nonstick parchment paper. Bake in a preheated oven, 375°F, for 4–5 minutes until golden brown. Allow to harden for 1–2 minutes then loosen and transfer to a cooling rack.

Melt the semisweet and the white chocolate in separate heatproof bowls set over saucepans of gently simmering water.

Hold a cookie over one of the bowls and spoon a little of the chocolate over half of it, spreading it with the back of the spoon. Return the cookie to the cooling rack and coat all the cookies in the same way, so half are covered with dark and the rest in white chocolate. Leave in a cool place for 30 minutes until the chocolate has hardened. Store in an airtight container, the layers separated with sheets of nonstick or waxed paper, for up to 2 days.

For honey cookies, use honey instead of the maple syrup, and ground ginger in place of the ground cinnamon. Sprinkle brown sugar over the cookies just before cooking, instead of coating them in melted chocolate afterwards.

almond shorties

Makes **14**
Preparation time **25 minutes**
Cooking time **15 minutes**

1½ cups **all-purpose flour**
½ cup **ground almonds**
¼ cup **superfine sugar**
a few drops of **almond
    extract**
⅔ cup **butter**, diced

To decorate
3 tablespoons **whole
    blanched almonds**, halved
2 **candied cherries**, cut into
    small pieces
extra **superfine sugar**,
    for sprinkling

Put the flour, ground almonds, sugar, and almond extract in a mixing bowl or a food processor. Add the butter and blend with your fingertips or process until the mixture resembles fine bread crumbs.

Squeeze the mixture together with your hands to form a ball. Knead lightly then roll out on a lightly floured surface until ½ inch thick. Stamp out 2½ inch circles using a fluted round cookie cutter. Transfer to an ungreased cookie sheet. Reknead the trimmings and continue rolling and stamping out until all the mixture has been used.

Prick each shortbread cookie 4 times with a fork to make a cross shape then add an almond half to the space between each fork mark. Decorate the center with a small piece of candied cherry. Sprinkle with a little extra superfine sugar and bake in a preheated oven, 325°F, for about 15 minutes until pale golden.

Loosen the cookies and allow to cool on the cookie sheet or transfer to a cooling rack if preferred.

For orange flower shorties, omit the ground almonds from the shortie mixture and reduce the quantity of butter to ½ cup, adding 2 teaspoons orange flower water, or to taste. Bake as above then dust with sifted confectioners' sugar. Serve the cookies on their own or as an accompaniment to fruit fools or mousses.

linzer cookies

Makes **16**
Preparation time **35 minutes**
Cooking time **16 minutes**

½ cup **hazelnuts**
2 cups **all-purpose flour**
⅓ cup **superfine sugar**
⅔ cup **butter**, diced
finely grated zest of ½ **lemon**
1 **egg yolk**
4 tablespoons **raspberry jelly**
sifted **confectioners' sugar**,
  for dusting

Grind the hazelnuts very finely in a blender or coffee grinder. Set aside.

Put the flour and sugar in a mixing bowl or a food processor. Add the butter and blend with your fingertips or process until the mixture resembles fine bread crumbs. Stir in the ground hazelnuts and lemon zest, then mix in the egg yolk and bring the mixture together with your hands to form a firm dough.

Knead lightly then roll out half of the dough on a lightly floured surface until ½ inch thick. Stamp out 2¼ inch circles using a fluted round cookie cutter. Transfer to an ungreased cookie sheet. Use a small heart- or star-shaped cookie cutter to remove 1 inch hearts or stars from the middle of half of the cookies.

Bake the first cookies in a preheated oven, 350°F, for about 8 minutes, until pale golden brown, then repeat for the remaining dough.

Allow the cookies to harden for 1–2 minutes then loosen and transfer to a cooling rack to cool.

Divide the jelly evenly among the centers of the whole cookies and spread thickly, leaving a border of cookie showing. Cover with the hole-cut cookies, dust with a little sifted confectioners' sugar, and allow to cool completely before serving.

For orange & apricot sandwich cookies, add the grated zest of ½ small orange, instead of the lemon, and sandwich the cookies together with apricot jelly as above.

christmas tree decorations

Makes **20**
Preparation time **35 minutes,
  plus chilling**
Cooking time **10–12 minutes**

½ cup **butter**, at room
  temperature
½ cup **superfine sugar**
2 **egg yolks**
1 tablespoon **cocoa powder**
1 teaspoon **ground cinnamon**
1½ cups **all-purpose flour**

For the icing
1⅓ cups **confectioners'
  sugar**, sifted
4–5 teaspoons **egg white**
  or **water**

Beat the butter and sugar together in a mixing bowl
until pale and creamy. Stir in the egg yolks, cocoa
powder, and cinnamon then gradually mix in the flour
to form a smooth soft dough. Chill for 15 minutes.

Roll out the dough between 2 sheets of nonstick
parchment paper until ¼ inch thick. Stamp out festive
shapes using cookie cutters about 3 inches in diameter.
Transfer to greased cookie sheets. Reknead the
trimmings and continue rolling and stamping out until
all the mixture has been used.

Make a small hole in each cookie using the handle of
a teaspoon then bake at 350°F, for 10–12 minutes
until lightly browned. Remake the hole in each cookie
then allow to cool on the cookie sheets.

Mix the confectioners' sugar and the egg white or
water to a smooth thick icing. Spoon into a waxed
paper pastry bag, snip off the tip and pipe lines, dots,
and swirls to decorate the cookies. Allow to harden then
thread narrow ribbons through the holes and hang on
the Christmas tree or on white painted twigs standing
in a pitcher.

For orange & mixed spice hearts, follow the
recipe above but omit the cocoa powder, add an
extra tablespoon of flour and stir in the grated zest
of 1 small orange. Replace the ground cinnamon
with 1 teaspoon ground mixed spice. Cut out heart-
shaped cookies from the dough, make ribbon holes
in them, bake and decorate as above.

classic shortbread

Makes **16**
Preparation time **15 minutes,**
  plus chilling
Cooking time **18–20 minutes**

1 cup **unsalted butter**, at
  room temperature
½ cup **superfine sugar**, plus
  extra for sprinkling
2 cups **all-purpose flour**
¾ cup **rice flour**
pinch of **salt**

Beat the butter and sugar together in a mixing bowl or a food processor until pale and creamy. Sift in the flour, rice flour, and salt and mix or process briefly until the ingredients just come together.

Transfer to a work surface and knead lightly to form a soft dough. Shape into a disk, wrap in plastic wrap and chill for 30 minutes.

Divide the dough in half and roll out each piece on a lightly floured surface to an 8 inch round. Transfer to 2 ungreased cookie sheets. Score each round with a sharp knife, marking it into 8 equal wedges, prick with a fork, and use your fingers to flute the edges.

Sprinkle with a little superfine sugar and bake in a preheated oven, 375°F, for 18–20 minutes until golden. Remove from the oven and, while still hot, cut into wedges through the score marks. Allow to cool on the cookie sheet for 5 minutes then transfer to a cooling rack to cool. Store in an airtight container.

For pistachio shortbread, simply replace 6 tablespoons of the rice flour with ⅛ cup shelled and very finely chopped pistachio nuts. Continue the recipe as above.

chunky cherry fudge cookies

Makes **18**
Preparation time **15 minutes**
Cooking time **10–12 minutes**

⅓ cup **butter**, at room
   temperature
⅓ cup **superfine sugar**
⅓ cup **light brown sugar**
1 teaspoon **vanilla extract**
1 **egg**, beaten
1½ cups **self-rising flour**
4 oz or 4 **chocolate-covered
   fudge bars**, chopped
⅓ cup **candied cherries**,
   roughly chopped

Put the butter, sugars, and vanilla in a mixing bowl and beat together until pale and creamy. Stir in the egg and flour and mix until smooth.

Stir in the fudge and cherries then spoon 18 mounds on to 2 baking sheets lined with nonstick parchment paper, leaving space between for them to spread during cooking.

Bake in a preheated oven, 350°F, for 10–12 minutes until golden brown. Allow to harden for 1–2 minutes then loosen and transfer to a cooling rack to cool completely. These are best eaten on the day they are made.

For dark chocolate & pistachio cookies, add 4 oz diced, semisweet chocolate and ⅓ cup roughly chopped, shelled pistachio nuts instead of the fudge and cherries. Bake as above, then sandwich together in pairs with scoops of vanilla ice cream. Serve immediately.

triple chocolate pretzels

Makes **40**
Preparation time **30 minutes,
plus rising and setting**
Cooking time **6–8 minutes**

2 cups **white bread flour**
1 teaspoon **active dry yeast**
2 teaspoons **superfine sugar**
large pinch of **salt**
1 tablespoon melted **butter or
sunflower oil**
½ cup **warm water**
3 oz each **semisweet, white,
and milk chocolate**, broken
into pieces

For the glaze
2 tablespoons **water**
½ teaspoon **salt**

Mix the flour, yeast, sugar, and salt in a mixing bowl.
Add the melted butter or oil and gradually mix in the
warm water until you have a smooth dough. Knead
the dough for 5 minutes on a lightly floured surface
until smooth and elastic.

Cut the dough into quarters, then cut each quarter
into 10 smaller pieces. Shape each piece into a thin
rope about 8 inches long. Bend the rope so that it
forms a wide arc, then bring one of the ends round in
a loop and secure about halfway along the rope. Do
the same with the other end, looping it across the first
secured end.

Transfer the pretzels to 2 large greased cookie sheets.
Cover loosely with lightly oiled plastic wrap and leave in
a warm place for 30 minutes until well risen.

Make the glaze. Mix the water and salt in a bowl until
the salt has dissolved then brush this over the pretzels.
Bake in a preheated oven, 400°F, for 6–8 minutes
until golden brown. Transfer to a cooling rack to cool.

Melt the different chocolates in 3 separate heatproof
bowls set over saucepans of gently simmering water.
Drizzle random lines of dark chocolate over the
pretzels, using a spoon. Allow to harden then repeat
with the white and then the milk chocolate.

For classic pretzels, brush plain pretzels as soon
as they come out of the oven with a glaze made by
heating 2 teaspoons salt, ½ teaspoon superfine
sugar, and 2 tablespoons water in a saucepan
until dissolved.

triple chocolate cookies

Makes **20**
Preparation time **15 minutes**
Cooking time **8–10 minutes**

⅓ cup **butter**, at room
   temperature
¾ cup **light brown sugar**
1 **egg**
1¼ cups **self-rising flour**
2 tablespoons **cocoa powder**
4 oz **white chocolate**,
   chopped
4 oz **milk chocolate**, chopped

Beat the butter and sugar together in a mixing bowl until pale and creamy. Stir in the egg, flour, and cocoa powder and mix until smooth.

Stir in the chopped chocolate then spoon 20 mounds of the mixture onto 2 greased cookie sheets, leaving space between for them to spread during cooking.

Bake in a preheated oven, 350°F, for 8–10 minutes until lightly browned. Allow to harden for 1–2 minutes then loosen and transfer to a cooling rack to cool completely. These are best eaten on the day they are made.

For chocolate, vanilla, & hazelnut cookies, follow the basic recipe above but omit the cocoa powder and increase the quantity of self-rising flour to 1½ cups. Omit the white chocolate and add ⅓ cup roughly chopped hazelnuts and 1 teaspoon vanilla extract in its place.

shortcakes with elderflower cream

Makes **8**
Preparation time **20 minutes**
Cooking time **10–15 minutes**

2 cups **self-rising flour**
2 teaspoons **baking powder**
⅓ cup **unsalted butter**, diced
3 tablespoons **superfine
  sugar**
1 **egg**, lightly beaten
2–3 tablespoons **milk**
1 tablespoon **butter**, melted
1⅔ cups **strawberries**, hulled
  and sliced
confectioners' sugar, for
  dusting

For the elderflower cream
1¼ cups **heavy cream**
2 tablespoons **elderflower
  syrup or undiluted cordial**

Sift the flour and baking powder into a mixing bowl or a food processor. Add the butter and blend with your fingertips or process until the mixture resembles fine bread crumbs. Stir in the sugar. Gradually add the egg and milk and continue mixing until the mixture just comes together to form a dough.

Roll out the dough on a lightly floured surface until ½ inch thick. Stamp out 3 inch circles using a plain round cookie cutter. Transfer to a large, lightly oiled cookie sheet and brush each round with a little melted butter.

Bake in a preheated oven, 400°F, for 10–15 minutes until risen and golden. Remove from the oven and transfer to a cooling rack to cool. While they are still warm, carefully slice each cake in half horizontally and return to the rack to cool completely.

Make the elderflower cream. Put the cream and elderflower syrup in a mixing bowl and whip until thickened. Spread the cream over the base of each cake, top with sliced strawberries and the cake lids. Serve dusted with confectioners' sugar.

For raspberry & cream shortcakes, make the shortcakes as above. Fill them with the same amount of heavy cream, flavored with 2 tablespoons of confectioners' sugar. Top the cream with 2 cups raspberries and put the cake lids on the top.

chocolate & chili cookies

Makes **12**
Preparation time **20 minutes**
Cooking time **16–20 minutes**

1 cup **all-purpose flour**
1 tablespoon **cocoa powder**
1 teaspoon **baking powder**
½ teaspoon **baking soda**
½ teaspoon **ground cinnamon**
¼ cup **light brown sugar**
¼ cup **butter**, diced
¼ teaspoon **"lazy"**
   ready-chopped chili from a
   jar or **mild fresh chopped**
   red chili
2 tablespoons **corn syrup**
4 oz **semisweet chocolate**,
   finely chopped

Stir all the dry ingredients together in a bowl or a food processor. Add the butter and chili and rub in with your fingertips or process until the mixture resembles fine bread crumbs.

Add the syrup, then mix together first with a spoon then squeeze the crumbs together with your hands to form a ball.

Knead in the chopped chocolate then shape the dough into a log and slice into 12. Roll each piece into a ball and arrange on 2 large greased cookie sheets. Cook one baking sheet at a time in the center of a preheated oven, 350°F, for 8–10 minutes until browned and the tops are craggy.

Allow to cool for 1–2 minutes then loosen and transfer to a cooling rack. These cookies are best eaten on the day they are made and delicious served while still warm.

For chocolate & ginger cookies, make the cookies in the same way as above but use 2 tablespoons ready-chopped crystallized ginger instead of the chili and ground cinnamon.

peanut butter cookies

Makes **32**
Preparation time **10 minutes**
Cooking time **12 minutes**

½ cup **unsalted butter**, at
 room temperature
⅔ cup **brown sugar**
½ cup **chunky peanut butter**
1 **egg**, lightly beaten
1¼ cups **all-purpose flour**
½ teaspoon **baking powder**
½ cup **unsalted peanuts**

Beat the butter and sugar together in a mixing bowl or a food processor until pale and creamy. Add the peanut butter, egg, flour, and baking powder and stir together until combined. Stir in the peanuts.

Drop large teaspoonfuls of the mixture onto 3 large, lightly oiled cookie sheets, leaving 2 inch gaps between each for them to spread during cooking.

Flatten the mounds slightly and bake in a preheated oven, 375°F, for 12 minutes until golden around the edges. Allow to cool on the cookie sheets for 2 minutes then transfer to a cooling rack to cool completely.

For peanut butter & chocolate chip cookies, use only ¼ cup unsalted peanuts and add ⅓ cup milk chocolate chips. Then make and bake the cookies as above.

raisin & caraway cookies

Makes **14**
Preparation time **20 minutes**
Cooking time **8–10 minutes**

1¾ cups **all-purpose flour**
1 teaspoon **baking powder**
1 teaspoon **caraway seeds**,
  roughly crushed
grated zest of ½ **lemon**
⅓ cup **superfine sugar**, plus
  extra for sprinkling
⅓ cup **butter**, diced
⅓ cup **golden raisins**
1 **egg**, beaten
1–2 tablespoons **lowfat milk**

Mix the flour and baking powder together in a mixing bowl or a food processor then add the crushed seeds, lemon zest, and sugar. Add the butter and blend with your fingertips or process until the mixture resembles fine bread crumbs.

Stir in the golden raisins then the egg and enough milk to mix to a soft but not sticky dough.

Knead lightly then roll out on a lightly floured surface until ¼ inch thick. Stamp out 3 inch circles using a fluted round cookie cutter. Transfer to a greased cookie sheet. Reknead the trimmings and continue rolling and stamping out until all the dough has been used.

Prick the cookies with a fork then sprinkle with a little extra superfine sugar and bake in a preheated oven, 350°F, for 8–10 minutes until pale golden. Transfer to a cooling rack to cool. Store in an airtight container for up to 5 days.

For fennel & orange biscuits, replace the caraway seeds and lemon zest in the recipe above with 1 teaspoon roughly crushed fennel seeds and the grated zest of ½ small orange. Continue the recipe as above.

oat & ginger crunchies

Makes **25**
Preparation time **20 minutes**
Cooking time **24–30 minutes**

½ cup **butter**
1 tablespoon **corn syrup**
½ cup **superfine sugar**
1 teaspoon **baking soda**
1 teaspoon **ground ginger**
2 tablespoons **ready-chopped crystallized ginger**
⅔ cup **whole-wheat flour**
1¼ cups **rolled oats**

Put the butter, syrup, and sugar in a saucepan and heat gently, stirring until the butter has melted and the sugar dissolved. Remove the pan from the heat then stir in the baking soda, ground and chopped ginger. Add the flour and oats and mix well.

Spoon heaping teaspoons of the mixture onto 3 lightly greased cookie sheets, leaving a little space between for the cookies to spread during cooking.

Cook one cookie sheet at a time in the center of a preheated oven, 350°F, for 8–10 minutes until the cookies are craggy and golden. Allow to harden for 1–2 minutes then loosen and transfer to a cooling rack to cool. Store in an airtight container for up to 3 days.

For orange crunchies, omit the ground and crystallized ginger and use the grated zest of ½ small orange in their place. Continue the recipe as above.

lime, pistachio, & hazelnut biscotti

Makes **about 30**
Preparation time **20 minutes**
Cooking time **43–48 minutes,**
  plus cooling

2 **eggs**
½ cup **superfine sugar**
1¾ cups **all-purpose flour**
1½ cups **ground almonds or**
  hazelnuts
1 heaping teaspoon **baking**
  powder
grated zest of 2 **limes**
pinch of **salt**
⅓ cup **shelled pistachio nuts,**
  roughly chopped
¼ cup **hazelnuts,** chopped

Beat the eggs and sugar together in a mixing bowl until pale and frothy. Using a wooden spoon, slowly work in the flour, ground almonds or hazelnuts, baking powder, lime zest, and salt.

Add the chopped pistachios and hazelnuts and knead lightly to form a soft dough. Shape the dough into a thick log, about 10 inches long and 4 inches wide, then flatten it slightly with the palm of your hand.

Transfer the dough to a greased cookie sheet and bake in a preheated oven, 350°F, for 35–40 minutes until light golden. Remove from the oven and allow to cool for 5 minutes, then cut into ¼ inch thick slices using a serrated knife.

Arrange the biscotti directly on a broiler pan and cook under a preheated low broiler for about 4 minutes on each side until crisp and golden. Transfer to a cooling rack to cool.

For lemon & macadamia biscotti, add the grated zest of 1 lemon in place of the lime zest and ½ cup macadamia nuts in place of the pistachio and hazelnuts. Continue the recipe as above.

coconut & pistachio cookies

Makes **20**
Preparation time **25 minutes,
  plus chilling**
Cooking time **8–10 minutes**

⅔ cup **butter**, at room
  temperature
⅔ cup **superfine sugar**
grated zest of **1 lime**
1 egg
⅔ cup **shredded coconut**
1¾ cups **all-purpose flour**
½ cup **shelled pistachio nuts**,
  finely chopped

Beat the butter and sugar together in a mixing bowl. Add the lime zest, egg, and coconut and beat until smooth. Gradually beat in the flour.

Spoon the mixture onto a piece of waxed paper and shape into a log about 14 inches long. Roll the dough in the chopped pistachios then wrap in the paper and twist the ends together. Chill in the refrigerator for at least 15 minutes or up to 3 days.

To serve, unwrap and slice off as many cookies as required. Arrange on a greased cookie sheet and bake in a preheated oven, 350°F, for 8–10 minutes until pale golden. Allow to cool for 5 minutes then transfer to a cooling rack to cool completely. These are best eaten on the day they are made.

For vanilla & demerara cookies, omit the lime and shredded coconut, and flavor the mixture with 1 teaspoon vanilla extract instead. Roll the dough in 4 tablespoons demerara sugar instead of the pistachios. Slice and bake as above.

traybakes

chocolate chip shortbread

Cuts into **12**
Preparation time **15 minutes**
Cooking time **20–25 minutes**

1 ¼ cups **all-purpose flour**
3 tablespoons **cornstarch**
½ cup **butter**, diced
¼ cup **superfine sugar**
3 oz **milk chocolate**, chopped

To finish
a little **ground cinnamon**
1 tablespoon **superfine sugar**

Put the flour and cornstarch in a mixing bowl or a food processor. Add the butter and blend with your fingertips or process until the mixture resembles fine bread crumbs. Stir in the sugar and chocolate then squeeze the crumbs together with your hands to form a ball.

Press into an ungreased 7 inch shallow square cake pan and prick the top with a fork. Mix the cinnamon and sugar together and sprinkle half over the top. Bake in a preheated oven, 325°F, for 20–25 minutes until pale golden.

Remove from the oven and mark into 12 bars. Sprinkle with the remaining cinnamon sugar mix and allow to cool in the pan. Cut the shortbread right through and lift out of the pan. Store in an airtight container for up to 5 days.

For lemon shortbread fingers, add the grated zest of 1 lemon to the flour and omit the milk chocolate and ground cinnamon. Press the shortbread mixture into the shallow square cake pan and bake as above.

jim jams

Cuts into **9**
Preparation time **10 minutes**
Cooking time **15–20 minutes**

½ cup **butter**
⅓ cup **corn syrup**
½ cup **light brown sugar**
1¼ cups **rolled oats**
¾ cup **self-rising whole-wheat flour**
⅓ cup **shredded coconut**

To finish
3 tablespoons **strawberry jelly**
2 tablespoons **shredded coconut**

Put the butter, syrup, and sugar in a saucepan and heat gently until just melted.

Remove the pan from the heat and stir in the oats, flour, and coconut. Tip the mixture into a 7 inch shallow square cake pan lined with nonstick parchment paper (see page 11), and press into an even layer.

Bake in a preheated oven, 350°F, for 15–20 minutes until golden. Allow to cool for 10 minutes then mark into 9 squares. Spread with the jelly and sprinkle with the coconut. Allow to cool completely.

Lift the paper out of the pan cut the squares right through and peel off the paper. Store in an airtight container for up to 3 days.

For marmalade squares, stir 2 tablespoons chunky marmalade into the mixture before spooning it into the prepared cake pan and baking as above. To finish, glaze with a little extra marmalade when the pan comes out of the oven and omit the shredded coconut. Cut into squares.

power bars

Cuts into **16**
Preparation **15 minutes**
Cooking time **25–30 minutes**

1 cup **butter**

⅔ cup **light brown sugar**

4 tablespoons **corn syrup**

¾ cup **mixed seeds** (such as
sesame, sunflower, pumpkin,
hemp, and light or dark flax
seeds)

⅓ cup **whole unblanched
almonds**

½ cup **hazelnuts**

1 **dessert apple**, cored, diced
but not peeled

1 small **banana**, peeled and
roughly mashed

2 cups **rolled oats**

Put the butter, sugar, and syrup in a saucepan and
heat gently until just melted. Remove the pan from the
heat and stir in all the remaining ingredients. Tip the
mixture into a 7 x 11 inch roasting pan lined with
nonstick parchment paper (see page 11), and press
into an even layer.

Bake in a preheated oven, 350°F, for 25–30 minutes
until golden brown and just beginning to darken
around the edges. Allow to cool for 10 minutes then
mark into 16 bars and allow to cool completely.

Lift the paper out of the pan, cut the bars right
through and peel off the paper. Store in an airtight
container for up to 3 days—they are energy boosters
and therefore ideal for adding to lunchboxes.

For sesame & banana squares, melt the butter,
sugar, and syrup as above, then stir in 6 tablespoons
sesame seeds instead of the mixed seeds. Omit
the nuts and apple and mix in 2 small peeled and
mashed bananas and 2½ cups rolled oats. Spoon
into an 8 inch shallow cake pan with base and sides
lined with nonstick parchment paper snipped into the
corners. Bake for 25 minutes until golden. Cool, then
cut into 16 small squares.

cherry & almond cornmeal cake

Cuts into **14**
Preparation time **25 minutes**
Cooking time **25–30 minutes**

¾ cup **butter**, at room
  temperature
¾ cup **superfine sugar**
3 **eggs**, beaten
½ cup **"1 minute cook"**
  yellow cornmeal
1 cup **ground almonds**
1 teaspoon **baking powder**
grated zest and juice of
  ½ **lemon**
14 oz can **pitted black**
  cherries, drained
2½ tablespoons **slivered**
  almonds
sifted **confectioners' sugar**,
  to decorate

Beat the butter and sugar together in a mixing bowl until pale and creamy. Gradually mix in alternate spoonfuls of beaten egg and cornmeal. Stir in the ground almonds and baking powder then mix in the lemon zest and juice.

Spoon the mixture into a greased 7 x 11 inch roasting pan. Sprinkle the canned cherries over the top then the slivered almonds.

Bake in a preheated oven, 350°F, for 25–30 minutes until well risen, the cake is golden and springs back when gently pressed with a fingertip.

Allow to cool in the pan, dust with sifted confectioners' sugar then cut into 14 bars and lift out of the pan. Store in an airtight container for up to 2 days.

For plum & hazelnut cornmeal cake, replace the ground almonds with ¾ cup toasted and very finely chopped hazelnuts and top with 13 oz red plums, pitted and sliced, instead of the canned cherries. Sprinkle some untoasted hazelnuts over the top instead of slivered almonds and bake as above.

rum & raisin chocolate brownies

Cuts into **20**
Preparation time **30 minutes,
  plus soaking**
Cooking time **25–30 minutes**

3 tablespoons **white or
  dark rum**
⅔ cup **raisins**
8 oz **semisweet chocolate,**
  broken into pieces
1 cup **butter**
4 **eggs**
1 cup **superfine sugar**
¾ cup **self-rising flour**
1 teaspoon **baking powder**
4 oz **white or milk chocolate**

Warm the rum, add the raisins and allow to soak for
2 hours or overnight.

Heat the semisweet chocolate and butter gently in a
saucepan until both have melted. Meanwhile, beat the
eggs and sugar together in a bowl, using an electric
beater, until very thick and the beater leaves a trail when
lifted above the mixture.

Fold the warm chocolate and butter into the beaten
eggs and sugar. Sift the flour and baking powder over
the top then fold in. Pour the mixture into a 7 x 11 inch
roasting pan lined with nonstick parchment paper, and
ease into the corners. Spoon the rum-soaked raisins
over the top.

Bake in a preheated oven, 350°F, for 25–30 minutes
until well risen, the top is crusty and cracked and the
center still slightly soft. Allow to cool and harden in
the pan.

Lift out of the pan using the lining paper. Melt the milk
chocolate in a heatproof bowl set over a saucepan of
gently simmering water then drizzle over the top of the
brownies. Allow to harden then cut into 20 pieces. Peel
off the paper and store in an airtight container for up to
3 days.

For triple chocolate brownies, omit the rum-soaked
raisins and instead sprinkle 4 oz finely chopped milk
chocolate and 4 oz finely chopped white chocolate
over the mixture just before baking. Bake as above
then omit the melted chocolate topping.

white chocolate & apricot blondies

Cuts into **20**
Preparation time **25 minutes**
Cooking time **25–30 minutes**

10 oz **white chocolate**
½ cup **butter**
3 **eggs**
¾ cup **superfine sugar**
1 teaspoon **vanilla extract**
1½ cups **self-rising flour**
1 teaspoon **baking powder**
¾ cup **ready-to-eat dried apricots**, chopped

Break half the chocolate into pieces, place in a saucepan with the butter and heat gently until melted. Dice the remaining chocolate.

Beat the eggs, sugar, and vanilla together in a bowl, using an electric beater, for about 5 minutes until very thick and foamy and the beater leaves a trail when lifted above the mixture. Fold in the melted chocolate mixture and then the flour and baking powder. Gently fold in half the chopped chocolate and apricots.

Pour the mixture into a 7 x 11 inch roasting pan lined with nonstick parchment paper, and ease into the corners. Sprinkle with the remaining chocolate and apricots. Bake in a preheated oven, 350°F, for 25–30 minutes until well risen, the top is crusty and the center still slightly soft.

Allow to cool in the pan then lift out using the lining paper and cut into 20 small pieces. Peel off the paper and store in an airtight container for up to 3 days.

For white chocolate & cranberry blondies, follow the recipe above, simply replacing the ready-to-eat dried apricots with ⅔ cup dried cranberries.

tropical gingercake

Cuts into **20**
Preparation time **30 minutes**
Cooking time **25 minutes**

⅔ cup **butter**
½ cup **light brown sugar**
3 tablespoons **corn syrup**
2 cups **self-rising flour**
1 teaspoon **baking powder**
3 teaspoons **ground ginger**
⅔ cup **shredded coconut**
3 **eggs**, beaten
7 oz can **pineapple rings**,
   drained and chopped

For the lime frosting
½ cup **butter**, at room
   temperature
1¾ cups sifted **confectioners'**
   sugar
grated zest and juice of **1 lime**
ready-to-eat dried papaya
   and apricot, diced
few **dried coconut** shavings,
   for sprinkling

Heat the butter, sugar, and syrup gently in a saucepan, stirring until melted.

Mix the dry ingredients together in a mixing bowl then stir in the melted butter mixture and beat together until smooth. Stir in the eggs then the chopped pineapple, reserving a few pieces for decoration if desired.

Pour the mixture into a 7 x 11 inch roasting pan, greased and base-lined with oiled waxed paper, and spread the surface level.

Bake in a preheated oven, 350°F, for about 20 minutes until well risen and the cake springs back when gently pressed with a fingertip. Allow to cool in the pan for 10 minutes then loosen the edges, turn out onto a cooling rack and peel off the lining paper.

Make the lime frosting. Beat the butter, confectioners' sugar, half the lime zest, and juice together to a smooth fluffy mixture. Turn the cake over so the top is uppermost then spread with the lime frosting. Decorate with a sprinkling of the remaining lime zest, the ready-to-eat dried fruits, and coconut shavings. Store in an airtight container for up to 2 days. Cut into 20 pieces to serve.

For carrot & raisin cake, follow the above recipe but omit the ground ginger. Add 1 cup peeled and grated carrots and ½ cup golden raisins in place of the pineapple and the shredded coconut. Use the grated zest and juice of ½ small orange in the frosting instead of the lime.

chocolate pear & orange squares

Cuts into **8**
Preparation time **25 minutes**
Cooking time **30–35 minutes**

¾ cup **butter**, at room
   temperature
¾ cup **superfine sugar**
3 **eggs**, beaten
1 cup **self-rising flour**
½ cup **self-rising whole-
   wheat flour**
¼ cup **cocoa**
grated zest and 2 tablespoons
   juice from 1 **orange**
4 small **pears**, peeled, halved,
   and cored

To finish
sifted **confectioners' sugar**,
   for dusting
a little grated **chocolate**
a little grated **orange zest**

Beat the butter and sugar together in a mixing bowl until light and fluffy. Gradually mix in alternate spoonfuls of beaten egg and flour until all has been added and the mixture is smooth. Stir in the cocoa, orange zest, and juice then spoon the mixture into a 7 x 11 inch roasting pan lined with nonstick parchment paper (see page 11), and spread the surface level.

Cut each pear half into long thin slices and fan out slightly but keep together in their original shape. Carefully lift onto the top of the cake and arrange in 2 rows of 4.

Bake in a preheated oven, 350°F, for 30–35 minutes until well risen and the cake springs back when gently pressed with a fingertip.

Lift out of the pan using the lining paper, cut into 8 pieces and peel off the paper. Dust with sifted confectioners' sugar and sprinkle with a little extra grated chocolate and orange zest. Serve warm or cold as it is, or serve it warm as a dessert with ice cream or custard. Store in an airtight container for up to 2 days.

For honeyed pear squares, replace the superfine sugar with ½ cup thick honey. Omit the cocoa and add ¾ cup self-rising whole-wheat flour. Drizzle the pears in the baked cake with a little honey and then dust with sifted confectioners' sugar.

apple & blackberry crumble cake

Cuts into **16**
Preparation time **30 minutes**
Cooking time **45 minutes**

¾ cup **butter**, at room
   temperature
¾ cup **superfine sugar**
3 **eggs**, beaten
1¾ cups **self-rising flour**
1 teaspoon **baking powder**
grated zest of **1 lemon**
1 lb **cooking apples**, cored,
   peeled, and thinly sliced
1 cup **frozen blackberries**,
   just defrosted

For the crumble topping
¾ cup **self-rising flour**
1 cup **granola**
¼ cup **superfine sugar**
⅓ cup **butter**, diced

Cream the butter and sugar together in a mixing bowl until pale and creamy. Gradually mix in alternate spoonfuls of beaten egg and flour until all has been added and the mixture is smooth. Stir in the baking powder and lemon zest then spoon the mixture into a 7 x 11 inch roasting pan lined with nonstick parchment paper (see page 11). Spread the surface level then arrange the apple slices and blackberries over the top.

Make the crumble topping. Put the flour, granola, and superfine sugar in a mixing bowl, add the butter and blend with your fingertips until the mixture resembles fine bread crumbs. Sprinkle over the top of the fruit. Bake in a preheated oven, 350°F, for about 45 minutes until the crumble is golden brown and a toothpick inserted into the center comes out clean.

Allow to cool in the pan then lift out using the lining paper. Cut the cake into 16 bars and peel off the lining paper. Store in an airtight container for up to 2 days.

For apple & mincemeat crumble cake, replace the frozen blackberries with ½ cup mincemeat. Sprinkle with crumble topping then add ¼ cup slivered almonds. Bake as above.

frosted banana bars

Cuts into **16**
Preparation time **30 minutes**
Cooking time **25–30 minutes**

¾ cup **butter**, at room
   temperature
¾ cup **superfine sugar**
3 **eggs**, beaten
2 cups **self-rising flour**
1 teaspoon **baking powder**
2 **bananas**, about 6 oz each
   with skins on, peeled and
   roughly mashed

For the frosting
¼ cup **butter**
¼ cup **cocoa powder**
2¼ cups **confectioners'
   sugar**, sifted
1–2 tablespoons **milk**
sugar shapes and sprinkles,
   to decorate

Cream the butter and sugar together in a mixing bowl until pale and creamy. Gradually mix in alternate spoonfuls of beaten egg and flour until all has been added and the mixture is smooth. Add the baking powder and mashed bananas and mix well.

Spoon the mixture into a 7 x 11 inch roasting pan lined with nonstick parchment paper, and spread the surface level. Bake in a preheated oven, 350°F, for 25–30 minutes until well risen, the cake is golden and springs back when gently pressed with a fingertip. Allow to cool in the pan.

Make the frosting. Heat the butter in a small saucepan. Stir in the cocoa powder and cook gently for 1 minute then remove the pan from the heat and mix in the confectioners' sugar. Return to the heat and heat gently, stirring until melted and smooth, adding enough milk to mix to a smooth spreadable frosting.

Pour the frosting over the top of the cake and spread the surface level with a spatula. Sprinkle with sugar shapes and sprinkles and allow to cool and harden. Lift the cake out of the pan using the lining paper. Cut into 16 bars and peel off the paper. Store in an airtight container for up to 3 days.

For cranberry & banana bites, stir 6 tablespoons dried cranberries into the cake mix along with the mashed bananas. Spoon into the pan as above and sprinkle with 4 tablespoons sunflower seeds. Bake, then dust with a little sifted confectioners' sugar when cool. Cut into 24 squares.

mango & kiwi upside down cakes

Cuts into **20**
Preparation time **30 minutes**
Cooking time **30–35 minutes**

1 large **mango**
4 tablespoons **apricot jelly**
grated zest and juice of 2
  limes
2 **kiwi fruit**, sliced
1 cup **soft margarine**
½ cup **superfine sugar**
½ cup **light brown sugar**
2 cups **self-rising flour**
4 **eggs**

Cut a thick slice off each side of the mango to reveal the large flat central pit. Cut the flesh away from the pit then peel and slice.

Mix the apricot jelly with the juice of 1 of the limes then spoon into the base of a 7 x 11 inch roasting pan lined with nonstick parchment paper (see page 11). Arrange the mango and kiwi fruit randomly over the top.

Put the lime zest and rest of the juice in a mixing bowl or a food processor, add the remaining ingredients, and beat until smooth. Spoon over the top of the fruit and spread the surface level. Bake in a preheated oven, 350°F, for 30–35 minutes until well risen, the cake is golden and springs back when gently pressed with a fingertip.

Allow to cool in the pan for 10 minutes then invert the pan onto a cooling rack, remove the pan and lining paper, and allow to cool completely. Cut into 20 pieces and serve warm with whipped cream. This is best eaten on the day it is made.

For apricot & cranberry upside down cakes, spoon cranberry sauce over the base of the pan instead of the apricot jelly. Cover with a 14 oz can apricot halves, drained and arranged in rows, instead of the fresh fruit. Replace the lime zest and juice from the cake mixture with the grated zest of 1 orange. Top the fruit with the cake mixture and bake as above.

prune & sunflower squares

Cuts into **16**
Preparation time **25 minutes**
Cooking time **30–35 minutes**

1½ cups **ready-to-eat pitted prunes**, roughly chopped
1 teaspoon **vanilla extract**
¾ cup **water**
⅔ cup **butter**
½ cup **superfine sugar**
2 tablespoons **corn syrup**
1 cup **self-rising flour**
1½ cups **rolled oats**
¼ cup **sunflower seeds**

To finish
3 tablespoons **rolled oats**
2 tablespoons **sunflower seeds**

Put the prunes, vanilla, and water in a small saucepan. Simmer, uncovered, for 5 minutes until soft and pulpy and the water has been absorbed.

Heat the butter, sugar, and syrup in a larger saucepan until melted. Stir in the flour, oats, and seeds and mix until well combined.

Spoon three-quarters of the mixture into an 8 inch shallow square cake pan lined with nonstick parchment paper (see page 11). Press into an even layer then cover with the cooked prunes. Sprinkle the remaining oat mixture over the top in a thin layer then decorate with the extra oats and sunflower seeds. Bake in a preheated oven, 350°F, for 25–30 minutes until golden brown.

Allow to cool in the pan for 10 minutes then mark into 16 squares and allow to cool completely. Lift out of the pan using the lining paper, peel off the paper and separate the squares. Store in an airtight container for up to 3 days.

For date & apple squares, instead of using the prunes and vanilla, cook 1 cup ready-chopped dates with 1 cored and chopped dessert apple in the same amount of water as above. Strain any excess liquid before spooning over the oat mixture. Continue the recipe as above.

chocolate caramel shortbread

Cuts into **15**
Preparation time **20 minutes,
plus chilling**
Cooking time **15 minutes**

½ cup **butter**, at room
temperature
¼ cup **superfine sugar**
½ cup **brown rice flour**
⅔ cup **cornstarch**

For the caramel
½ cup **butter**
¼ cup **light brown sugar**
1 cup **condensed milk**

For the topping
4 oz **white chocolate**, broken
into pieces
4 oz **semisweet chocolate**,
broken into pieces

Beat the butter and sugar together in a mixing bowl until pale and creamy, then stir in the flours until well combined. Press the shortbread into an 11 x 7 inch baking pan, then place in a preheated oven, 400°F, for 10–12 minutes until golden.

Meanwhile, place the caramel ingredients in a heavy saucepan and heat over a low heat until the sugar has dissolved, then cook for 5 minutes, stirring continuously until just beginning to darken. Remove from the heat and allow to cool a little, then pour the caramel over the shortbread base and allow to cool completely.

Melt the white and semisweet chocolate in separate heatproof bowls set over saucepans of simmering water. When the caramel is firm, spoon alternate spoonfuls of the white and dark chocolate over the caramel, tap the pan on the work surface so that the different chocolates merge, then use a knife to make swirls in the chocolate. Refrigerate until set, then cut into 15 pieces.

For caramel pine nut slice, make the shortbread base as above, adding the grated zest of ½ orange along with the flour. Bake as above. Stir ⅛ cup pine nuts into the caramel just before pouring over the shortbread. When cool, decorate with 4 oz melted semisweet chocolate drizzled randomly over the top so that the caramel can still be seen.

centerpiece cakes

strawberry macaroon cake

Cuts into **8**
Preparation time **40 minutes**
Cooking time **35–45 minutes**

4 **egg whites**
¼ teaspoon **cream of tartar**
½ cup **light brown sugar**
½ cup **superfine sugar**
1 teaspoon **white wine vinegar**
⅓ cup **walnut pieces**, lightly toasted and chopped

For the filling
¾ cup **heavy cream**
1⅔ cups **strawberries**

Beat the egg whites and cream of tartar in a large clean bowl until stiff. Combine the sugars then gradually beat into the egg white, a little at a time, until it has all been added. Beat for a few minutes more until the meringue mixture is thick and glossy. Fold in the walnuts.

Divide the meringue mixture evenly between 2 greased 8 inch layer pans, base-lined with nonstick parchment paper. Spread the surfaces level then swirl the tops with the back of a spoon. Bake in a preheated oven, 300°F, for 35–45 minutes until lightly browned and crisp. Loosen the edges and allow to cool in the pans.

Re-loosen the edges of the meringues and turn out on to 2 clean dish towels. Peel off the lining paper then put one of the meringues on a serving plate.

Whip the cream until softly peaking then spoon three-quarters over the meringue. Halve 8 of the smallest strawberries and set aside. Hull and slice the rest and arrange on the cream. Cover with the second meringue, top uppermost. Decorate with spoonfuls of the remaining cream and the reserved halved strawberries. Serve within 2 hours of assembly.

For chocolate & chestnut macaroon cake, fold 2 tablespoons cocoa powder into the meringue mixture just before adding the nuts. Bake as above then replace the strawberries and cream filling with ⅔ cup heavy cream, whipped and folded with a 7½ oz can sweetened chestnut puree. Decorate the top with chocolate curls.

chocolate & rum cake

Cuts into **16**
Preparation time **15 minutes**
Cooking time **25–30 minutes**

5 oz **semisweet chocolate**,
 broken into pieces
grated zest and juice of
 1 orange
a few drops of **rum extract**
 (optional)
⅔ cup **unsalted butter**, at
 room temperature
⅔ cup **superfine sugar**
4 **eggs**, separated
1¼ cups **ground almonds**

For the chocolate frosting
5 oz **semisweet chocolate**,
 broken into pieces
½ cup **unsalted butter**

To decorate
8–16 **crystallized violet
 petals** (optional)

Melt together the chocolate, orange zest and juice, and rum extract, if using, in a heatproof bowl set over a saucepan of gently simmering water.

Place the butter and all but 1 tablespoon of the sugar in a large mixing bowl and beat together until pale and creamy. Beat in the egg yolks, one at a time, then stir in the melted chocolate.

Beat the egg whites in a large clean bowl until softly peaking. Add the remaining sugar, then beat until stiff. Fold the egg whites into the chocolate mixture with the ground almonds, then spoon into 2 greased and base-lined 8 inch layer pans.

Bake in a preheated oven, 350°F, for 20–25 minutes, until the sides of the cakes are cooked but the centers are still a little unset. Remove from the oven, allow to cool in the pans for a few minutes then turn out gently onto a cooling rack.

Frost the cake. Melt the chocolate as before then beat in the butter, a tablespoon at a time, until melted. Remove from the heat and beat occasionally until cool. If the frosting is runny, put the bowl in the refrigerator until it firms up a little. Fill and frost the cooled cake with the chocolate mixture. Decorate with crystallized violet petals, if desired.

For orange liqueur cake, omit the rum. Make the cake as above, then sandwich and top it with ¾ cup whipped heavy cream flavored with 2 tablespoons Cointreau and 2 tablespoons confectioners' sugar. Decorate with fresh orange segments.

138

apple sauce cake

Cuts into **8**
Preparation time **30 minutes**
Cooking time **40–45 minutes**

2 **cooking apples**, about
   8 oz each, cored, peeled,
   and thinly sliced
2 tablespoons **water**
a little **lemon juice**
2 cups **white bread flour**
2½ teaspoons **baking powder**
1 teaspoon **ground cinnamon**
½ teaspoon **ground ginger**
¼ teaspoon **grated nutmeg**
⅔ cup **reduced-fat spread**
¾ cup **superfine sugar**
3 **eggs**, beaten

Put half the apple slices in a small saucepan with the water, then cover and simmer for 5 minutes until pulpy. Put the remaining apple slices in a bowl of cold water with a little lemon juice.

Mix the flour, baking powder, half the ground cinnamon, and all of the ginger and nutmeg together in a mixing bowl.

Cream the reduced-fat spread with ⅔ cup sugar in another bowl. Gradually mix in alternate spoonfuls of beaten egg and flour mixture until all has been added and the mixture is smooth. Stir in the cooked apple.

Pour the mixture into a lightly oiled 9 inch springform cake pan and spread the surface level. Drain the remaining apples well and arrange the slices in rings on top of the cake mixture. Sprinkle with the remaining sugar and cinnamon. Bake in a preheated oven, 350°F, for 35–40 minutes until well risen and a toothpick inserted into the center comes out clean.

Serve the cake while still warm, on its own or as a dessert with sour cream, yogurt, or custard.

For spiced pear cake, make the cake replacing the apples with the same weight of pears, 1 teaspoon ground ginger and ½ teaspoon ground cinnamon, sprinkling half the ginger on the top of the cake with the sugar. Bake as above.

chocolate & sweet potato torte

Cuts into **12–14**

Preparation time **40 minutes**

Cooking time **40–45 minutes**

1¾ cups **self-rising flour**

½ cup **cocoa powder**

1 teaspoon **baking soda**

¾ cup **butter**

¾ cup **light brown sugar**

3 **eggs**, beaten

13 oz **sweet potato**, boiled, drained, and mashed with 3 tablespoons **milk**

¼ cup chopped **crystallized ginger**

For the frosting

5 oz **semisweet chocolate**

2 tablespoons **light brown sugar**

¾ cup **full-fat sour cream**

To decorate

3 tablespoons chopped **crystallized ginger**

a few **crystallized rose petals or violets** (see page 144)

Mix the flour, cocoa powder, and baking soda together in a bowl. Beat the butter and sugar together in a mixing bowl until pale and creamy. Gradually mix in alternate spoonfuls of beaten egg and flour mixture until all has been added and the mixture is smooth. Stir in the mashed sweet potato and ginger.

Pour the mixture into a 9 inch springform pan, greased and base-lined with oiled waxed paper, then spread the surface level. Bake in a preheated oven, 325°F, for 45–50 minutes until the cake has risen with a slightly domed and cracked top and a toothpick inserted into the center comes out clean.

Allow to cool in the pan for 15 minutes (don't worry if it sinks slightly) then turn out onto a wire rack and peel off the lining paper. Allow to cool completely.

Make the frosting. Melt the chocolate and brown sugar in a heatproof bowl set over a saucepan of gently simmering water. Remove from the heat, add the sour cream and stir until smooth and glossy. Chill for 10–30 minutes if needed, until the frosting is thick enough to spread. Spoon the chocolate frosting over the cake top and sides and swirl with a knife.

Sprinkle with the ginger and crystallized flower petals, if using, then leave in a cool place to set.

lemon angel food cake

Cuts into **8**
Preparation time **30 minutes**
Cooking time **25–30 minutes**

½ cup **all-purpose flour**
finely grated zest of ½ **lemon**
6 **egg whites**
pinch of **salt**
¾ teaspoon **cream of tartar**
1 cup **superfine sugar**
crystallized rose petals or
flowers, to decorate
(optional)

For the topping
½ cup **lemon curd**
½ cup **sour cream**

Sift the flour into a bowl, stir in the lemon zest, and set aside.

Beat the egg whites, salt, and cream of tartar in a large clean bowl until stiff but moist-looking. Gradually beat in the sugar, a tablespoonful at a time, until it has all been added. Beat for a few minutes more until the meringue mixture is thick and glossy.

Gently fold in the flour mixture using a metal spoon and a swirling figure-of-eight action. Pour into an 8 or 9 inch nonstick tube pan. Bake in a preheated oven, 375°F, for 25–30 minutes until well risen, the cake is golden and springs back when gently pressed with a fingertip.

Invert the pan onto a cooling rack and allow to cool. As it cools the cake will fall out of the pan. When cold, mix the lemon curd and sour cream together and spread over the top of the cake. Sprinkle with crystallized rose petals or flowers, if using.

To crystallize flowers such as rose petals or viola, pansy, or herb flowers, first make sure they are clean. Brush them with egg white then dust lightly with a little superfine sugar. Allow to dry for at least 30 minutes before using to decorate the cake.

For lime angel food cake with pistachios, replace the grated lemon zest with the finely grated zest of 1 lime and use lime curd in place of the lemon curd for the topping. Toast ¼ cup pistachio nuts with 1 tablespoon superfine sugar under a broiler until the sugar has dissolved and caramelized lightly, cool, then roughly chop and sprinkle over the cake.

144

plum & almond streusel cake

Cuts into **12**
Preparation time **35 minutes**
Cooking time **1 hour–1 hour
10 minutes**

For the streusel topping
¼ cup **self-rising flour**
2 tablespoons **superfine
sugar**
2 tablespoons **butter**, diced
⅓ cup **slivered almonds**

For the cake
¾ cup **butter**, at room
temperature
¾ cup **superfine sugar**
3 **eggs**, beaten
1½ cups **self-rising flour**
1 teaspoon **baking powder**
½ cup **ground almonds**
½ teaspoon **almond extract**
13 oz **red plums**, halved,
pitted, and thickly sliced
sifted **confectioners' sugar**,
to decorate

Make the streusel topping. Put the flour and sugar
in a small bowl. Add the butter and blend with your
fingertips until the mixture resembles fine bread
crumbs. Stir in the slivered almonds.

Make the cake. Beat the butter and sugar together in
a mixing bowl until pale and creamy. Gradually mix in
alternate spoonfuls of beaten egg and flour until all
has been added. Stir in the baking powder, ground
almonds, and almond extract.

Spoon the cake mixture into a 9 inch springform pan
lined with nonstick parchment paper over base and
sides, and spread the surface level. Arrange the sliced
plums randomly over the top then sprinkle with the
streusel topping.

Bake in a preheated oven, 350°F, for 1 hour–1 hour
10 minutes, or until a toothpick inserted into the
center comes out clean, covering the cake loosely with
foil halfway during cooking if the top appears to be
browning too quickly.

Allow to cool in the pan for 15 minutes then remove
the pan and allow the cake to cool completely. When
ready to serve, remove the lining paper and transfer to
a serving plate. Dust with sifted confectioners' sugar.
Cut into wedges and serve plain or serve while still
warm as a dessert with a spoonful of whipped cream
or vanilla ice cream. Eat within 2 days.

For peach melba streusel cake, follow the basic
recipe above but replace the plums with 2 sliced
fresh peaches and 1 cup raspberries.

cherub cake

Cuts into **8**
Preparation time 1½ **hours,**
    plus overnight drying
Cooking time **1–1¼ hours**

¾ cup **soft margarine**
¾ cup **superfine sugar**
3 **eggs**, beaten
2 cups **self-rising flour**
finely grated zest of 2 **limes**
juice of 1½ **limes**
½ cup **butter**, at room
    temperature
2¼ cups **confectioners'**
    sugar, plus extra for dusting
4 tablespoons **raspberry jelly**
1 lb **ready-to-use white icing**
8 oz **fondant**
edible **gold food coloring**
small tube **white decorator**
    frosting (optional)

Beat the margarine and sugar together in a bowl until pale and creamy. Mix in spoonfuls of the egg and flour until all has been added and the mixture is smooth.

Stir in the lime zest and the juice from ½ a lime. Spoon the mixture into an 8 inch deep round cake pan lined with nonstick parchment paper and spread the surface level. Bake in a preheated oven, 325°F, for 1–1¼ hours until well risen. Leave to cool in the pan then turn out. Peel off the lining paper and slice the cake horizontally into 3 layers.

Beat the butter, confectioners' sugar, and remaining lime juice together to make a smooth butter cream. Sandwich the cakes together using the butter cream and jelly. Spread the remaining mix thinly over the cake top and sides.

Drape the rolled icing over the cake. Gently press over the top and sides until smooth and trim away the excess icing. Press a small piece of fondant into a 2½ inch nonstick cherub icing mold. Invert the mold and gently ease out the shaped cherub. Trim and make another 3 cherubs.

Roll out the remaining fondant and cut into thin strips for the ribbons. Twist each one like a corkscrew over a wooden spoon handle and leave overnight to dry. Paint gold detail on the cherub wings. Arrange the cherubs on top of the cake, with the fondant ribbons. Secure with decorator frosting.

apricot & orange jelly roll

Cuts into **8**
Preparation time **30 minutes**
Cooking time **18–20 minutes**

For the filling
1¼ cups **ready-to-eat dried apricots**
¾ cup **apple juice**

For the sponge cake
4 **eggs**
½ cup **superfine sugar**, plus extra for sprinkling
grated zest of **1 orange**
1 cup **all-purpose flour**, sifted

Simmer the apricots and apple juice in a saucepan, covered, for 10 minutes or until most of the liquid has been absorbed. Puree then allow to cool.

Make the sponge cake. Put the eggs, sugar, and orange zest in a large heatproof bowl set over a saucepan of gently simmering water. Beat, using an electric beater, for 5–10 minutes until very thick and foamy and the beater leaves a trail when lifted above the mixture.

Gently fold in the sifted flour. Pour the mixture into a 12 x 9 inch roasting or jelly roll pan lined with nonstick parchment paper (see page 11), and ease into the corners. Bake in a preheated oven, 400°F, for 8–10 minutes until the cake is golden brown and just beginning to shrink away from the sides, and the top springs back when gently pressed with a fingertip.

Meanwhile, cover a clean damp dish towel with nonstick parchment paper and sprinkle with a little superfine sugar. Quickly turn out the sponge cake onto the sugared paper. Carefully peel off the lining paper. Spread the apricot puree over the cake then, starting with a short side and using the paper to help, roll up to form a log. Allow to cool and serve the same day.

For strawberry & almond roulade, sprinkle ⅓ cup slivered almonds over the paper-lined pan and flavor the cake mixture with ½ teaspoon almond extract instead of orange zest. Fill the roulade with 6 tablespoons strawberry jelly instead of the apricot puree and dust with sifted confectioners' sugar.

chocolate truffle cake

Cuts into **8**
Preparation time **15 minutes**
Cooking time **40 minutes**

8 oz **semisweet chocolate**,
  broken into pieces
½ cup **unsalted butter**
3 tablespoons **heavy cream**
4 **eggs**, separated
½ cup **superfine sugar**
2 tablespoons **cocoa powder**,
  sifted
confectioners' sugar,
  for dusting

Melt the chocolate, butter, and cream together in a heatproof bowl set over a saucepan of gently simmering water. Remove from the heat and allow to cool for 5 minutes.

Beat the egg yolks with three-quarters of the sugar until pale and stir in the cooled chocolate mixture.

Beat the egg whites in a large clean bowl until softly peaking then beat in the remaining sugar. Fold into the egg yolk mixture with the sifted cocoa powder until evenly incorporated.

Pour the cake mixture into an oiled and base-lined 9 inch springform cake pan that has been lightly dusted all over with a little extra cocoa powder. Bake in a preheated oven, 350°F, for 35 minutes.

Allow to cool in the pan for 10 minutes then turn out onto a serving plate. Serve in wedges, while still warm, with whipped cream and strawberries.

For chocolate & orange cake with brandied oranges, add the finely grated zest of 1 orange when folding in the confectioners' sugar above. Remove the rind from 3 oranges, cut them into segments, and soak in 3 tablespoons brandy and 1 tablespoon honey. Serve the oranges with the cake and spoon over sour cream.

st clements cake

Cuts into **8**
Preparation time **30 minutes**
Cooking time **20 minutes**

¾ cup **soft margarine**
¾ cup **superfine sugar**
1½ cups **self-rising flour**
1 teaspoon **baking powder**
3 **eggs**
finely grated zest of **1 lemon**
finely grated zest of **1 orange**
sifted **confectioners' sugar**,
  for dusting

For the filling
3 tablespoons **lemon curd**
⅔ cup **heavy cream**, whipped

Beat all of the cake ingredients in a mixing bowl or a food processor until smooth.

Spoon the cake mixture evenly into 2 greased and base-lined 7 inch layer pans and spread the surfaces level. Bake in a preheated oven, 350°F, for 20 minutes until well risen, the cake is golden brown and springs back when gently pressed with a fingertip.

Allow to cool in the pan for 5 minutes then loosen the edges, turn out onto a cooling rack and peel off the lining paper. Allow to cool.

Transfer one of the cakes to a serving plate and spread with the lemon curd. Spoon the whipped cream on top then cover with the remaining cake. Dust the top of the cake lightly with sifted confectioners' sugar. This is best eaten on the day it is made.

For chocolate & vanilla cake, omit the lemon and orange zest from the cake mixture and replace ¼ cup of the flour with the same amount of cocoa powder. Bake as above then fill with 3 tablespoons chocolate spread instead of lemon curd and ⅔ cup whipped heavy cream flavored with 1 teaspoon vanilla extract.

chocolate & chestnut roulade

Cuts into **8**
Preparation time **20 minutes,**
plus cooling
Cooking time **25 minutes**

4 oz **semisweet chocolate**
5 **eggs,** separated
¾ cup **superfine sugar,**
  plus extra for sprinkling
2 tablespoons **cocoa powder,**
  sifted
confectioners' sugar,
  for dusting

For the filling
1⅓ cups **unsweetened**
  chestnut puree
4 tablespoons **confectioners'**
  sugar
2 tablespoons **brandy**
1 cup **heavy cream**

Melt the chocolate in a heatproof bowl set over a saucepan of simmering water, stirring occasionally. Remove from the heat and allow to cool for 5 minutes.

Put the egg yolks in a bowl, add the sugar, and beat together for 5 minutes until pale and very thick. Stir in the melted chocolate and the cocoa powder. Beat the egg whites in a large clean bowl until stiff then fold into the chocolate mixture until evenly combined.

Transfer the mixture to an oiled and lined 13 x 9 inch jelly roll pan, easing it well into the corners and spreading the surface level with a spatula. Bake in a preheated oven, 350°F, for 20 minutes until risen and set.

Meanwhile, cover a clean damp dish towel with nonstick parchment paper and sprinkle with a little superfine sugar. Quickly turn out the cooked cake onto the paper. Carefully peel off the lining paper and cover the cake with a clean dish towel. Allow to cool.

Make the filling. Blend the chestnut puree and confectioners' sugar in a food processor until smooth. Transfer to a bowl and stir in the brandy. Slowly beat in the cream until light and fluffy. Spread the filling over the cake, leaving a ½ inch border all round. Starting with a short side and using the paper to help, roll up the cake to form a log. Dust with confectioners' sugar and serve.

chocolate & date layer cake

Cuts into **10**
Preparation time **30 minutes**
Cooking time **25 minutes**

¾ cup **ready-chopped dried dates**
⅔ cup **boiling water**, plus 6 tablespoons
½ cup **cocoa powder**
⅔ cup **sunflower oil**
3 **eggs**
¾ cup **superfine sugar**
1½ cups **self-rising flour**
1½ teaspoons **baking powder**

To finish
⅔ cup **heavy cream**
⅔ cup **plain yogurt**
3 tablespoons **chocolate spread**
5 bought **chocolate truffles,** halved

Simmer the dates in a saucepan with the ⅔ cup boiling water, covered, for 5 minutes until softened. Gradually mix the cocoa powder in a bowl with the remaining 6 tablespoons boiling water until smooth. Allow the dates and dissolved cocoa powder to cool.

Add the oil, eggs, and sugar to the dissolved cocoa powder then beat together until smooth. Add the flour and baking powder then beat again. Stir in the cooled dates and any cooking liquid and mix well.

Divide the mixture evenly between 2 x 8 inch layer pans, greased and base-lined with oiled waxed paper, and spread the surfaces level. Bake in a preheated oven, 350°F, for 20 minutes until well risen and the cakes spring back when gently pressed with a fingertip.

Allow to cool in the pans for 5 minutes then loosen the edges, turn out onto a cooling rack and peel off the lining paper. Allow to cool completely.

Whip the cream until softly peaking then fold in the yogurt. Put one cake onto a serving plate, spoon over chocolate spread then half the cream. Top with the second cake and spread with the remaining cream. Decorate with the halved chocolate truffles.

For black forest cake, make the cake as above but omit the dates. Drizzle each cooked cake with 2 tablespoons kirsch then fill with the whipped cream and yogurt, adding drained, pitted black cherries from a can to the middle and top of the cake.

coffee cake with pistachio praline

Cuts into **12**
Preparation time **40 minutes**
Cooking time **30–35 minutes**

6 **eggs**
¾ cup **superfine sugar**
1½ cups **all-purpose flour**,
   sifted
¼ cup **unsalted butter**, melted
2 tablespoons ready-made
   espresso coffee, cooled

For the praline
⅔ cup **shelled pistachio nuts**
½ cup **granulated sugar**
3 tablespoons **water**

**For the maple syrup
   frosting**
6 **egg yolks**
¾ cup **superfine sugar**
⅔ cup **milk**
1½ cups **unsalted butter**, at
   room temperature, diced
3 tablespoons **maple syrup**

Beat the eggs and sugar in a heatproof bowl set over
a saucepan of gently simmering water for 5 minutes
until very thick and the beater leaves a trail when lifted
above the mixture. Remove from the heat then fold in
the flour, butter, and coffee.

Transfer the mixture to an oiled and base-lined 9 inch
cake pan and bake in a preheated oven, 350°F, for
25–30 minutes. Allow to cool in the pan for 5 minutes
then turn out onto a cooling rack. Slice the cake
horizontally into 3 layers.

Put the nuts on a baking sheet. Heat the sugar and
water in a heavy saucepan until the sugar dissolves.
Increase the heat until the sugar turns light golden.
Remove from the heat and pour over the nuts. Once
set, break the praline into small pieces and then grind
to a rough powder.

Beat the egg yolks and sugar together until pale.
Heat the milk until just boiling, then beat into the egg
mixture. Return to the pan and heat gently, stirring,
until the mixture coats the back of the spoon. Beat
the mixture off the heat for 2–3 minutes and then
gradually beat in the butter, a little at a time, until the
mixture is thick and glossy. Beat in the maple syrup.

Fold half the praline into half the frosting and use to
sandwich the layers together. Spread the remaining
frosting over the top and sides of the cake and
sprinkle with the reserved praline.

For chocolate cake with hazelnut praline, substitute
¼ cup of the flour with cocoa powder and use shelled
hazelnuts in place of the pistachios.

blueberry meringue roulade

Cuts into **8**
Preparation time **30 minutes,
  plus cooling**
Cooking time **15 minutes**

4 **egg whites**
1 cup **superfine sugar**, plus
  extra for sprinkling
1 teaspoon **white wine
  vinegar**
1 teaspoon **cornstarch**

For the filling
grated zest of 1 **lime**
1¼ cups **heavy cream**,
  whipped
1⅓ cups **blueberries**
3 **passion fruit**, halved

Beat the egg whites in a large clean bowl until stiff.
Gradually beat in the sugar, a teaspoonful at time, until
it has all been added. Beat for a few minutes more until
the meringue mixture is thick and glossy.

Combine the vinegar and cornstarch then beat into the
meringue mixture. Spoon into a 13 x 9 inch jelly roll pan
lined with nonstick parchment paper that stands a little
above the top of the pan sides, then spread the surface
level. Bake in a preheated oven, 375°F, for 10 minutes
until pale brown and well risen, then reduce the heat to
325°F, for 5 minutes until just firm to the touch and the
top is slightly cracked.

Meanwhile, cover a clean dish towel with nonstick
parchment paper and sprinkle with a little superfine
sugar. Turn out the meringue onto the paper. Remove
the pan. Allow to cool for 1–2 hours. Carefully peel
off the lining paper.

Fold the lime zest into the whipped cream. Spread over
the meringue then sprinkle with the blueberries and
passion fruit seeds. Starting with a short side and using
the paper to help, roll up the meringue to form a log.
Serve the same day.

For minted strawberry roulade, spread the meringue
with whipped cream folded with a small bunch of
freshly chopped mint and 1⅔ cups roughly chopped
strawberries. Make the roulade as above and decorate
with halved baby strawberries and mint leaves dusted
with sifted confectioners' sugar.

family chocolate cake

Cuts into **8**
Preparation time **20 minutes,
 plus chilling**
Cooking time **30 minutes**

½ cup **superfine sugar**
4 **eggs**
1 cup **self-rising flour**
¼ cup **cocoa powder**
3 tablespoons **unsalted
 butter**, melted
1 teaspoon **vanilla extract**

For the frosting
12 oz **semisweet chocolate**,
 broken into pieces
1 cup **unsalted butter**
1 cup **confectioners' sugar**,
 sifted

Put the sugar and eggs in a heatproof bowl set over a saucepan of gently simmering water. Beat, using an electric beater, for 5–10 minutes until very thick and foamy and the beater leaves a trail when lifted above the mixture.

Sift over the flour and cocoa powder and carefully fold into the mixture with the melted butter and vanilla until well combined.

Pour the mixture into an oiled and base-lined 8 inch springform cake pan and bake in a preheated oven, 350°F, for 25 minutes until risen and firm to the touch. Remove from the oven and allow to cool in the pan for 5 minutes. Turn out onto a cooling rack and allow to cool.

Make the frosting. Melt the chocolate and butter together in a heatproof bowl set over a saucepan of gently simmering water. Remove from the heat and beat in the confectioners' sugar. Set aside to cool and then chill for 1 hour until thickened. Beat until pale and fluffy.

Slice the cake in half horizontally and use half of the frosting to sandwich the halves back together. Use the remaining frosting to cover the top and sides of the cake, swirling the mixture with a spatula.

For chocolate orange cake, add the finely grated zest of 1 orange to the sugar and eggs when beating and continue as above. Decorate the frosted cake with curls of orange peel.

old-fashioned coffee cake

Cuts into **8**
Preparation time **30 minutes**
Cooking time **20 minutes**

¾ cup **soft margarine**
¾ cup **light brown or
   superfine sugar**
1½ cups **self-rising flour**
1 teaspoon **baking powder**
3 **eggs**
3 teaspoons **instant coffee,**
   dissolved in 2 teaspoons
   boiling water

For the frosting
⅓ cup **butter**, at room
   temperature
1⅓ cups **confectioners'
   sugar**, sifted
3 teaspoons **instant coffee,**
   dissolved in 2 teaspoons
   boiling water
2 oz **semisweet chocolate,**
   melted

Beat all of the cake ingredients in a mixing bowl or a food processor until smooth.

Divide the mixture evenly between 2 x 7 inch layer pans, greased and base-lined with oiled waxed paper, and spread the surfaces level. Bake in a preheated oven, 350°F, for 20 minutes until well risen, the cakes are browned and spring back when gently pressed with a fingertip.

Leave the cakes for a few minutes then loosen the edges, turn out onto a cooling rack and peel off the lining paper. Allow to cool.

Make the frosting. Put the butter and half the confectioners' sugar in a mixing bowl, add the dissolved coffee, and beat until smooth. Gradually mix in the remaining confectioners' sugar until pale and creamy.

Put one of the cakes on a serving plate, spread with half the frosting then cover with the second cake. Spread the remaining frosting over the top. Pipe or drizzle swirls of melted chocolate on top. This cake can be stored in an airtight container for 2–3 days in a cool place.

For cinnamon & hazelnut cake, replace the dissolved coffee in the cake mixture with 1 teaspoon ground cinnamon and ⅓ cup toasted chopped hazelnuts. Use the maple frosting on page 168 to fill and cover the cake. Sprinkle with roughly chopped hazelnuts and dust with ground cinnamon to finish.

carrot & walnut cake

Cuts into **10**
Preparation time **40 minutes**
Cooking time **25 minutes**

⅔ cup **sunflower oil**
3 **eggs**
¾ cup **light brown sugar**
1½ cups **self-rising flour**
1½ teaspoons **baking powder**
grated zest of ½ **orange**
1 teaspoon **ground cinnamon**
1 cup coarsely grated **carrots**
½ cup **walnuts**, finely chopped

For the maple frosting
1 cup **maple syrup**
2 **egg whites**
pinch of **salt**

To decorate
5 **walnut halves**, halved

Put the oil, eggs, and sugar in a mixing bowl and beat together until smooth.

Add the flour, baking powder, orange zest, and ground cinnamon and beat again until smooth. Stir in the grated carrots and chopped nuts. Divide the mixture between 2 x 8 inch layer pans, waxed and base-lined with oiled greaseproof paper, and level.

Bake in a preheated oven, 350°F, for about 20 minutes until the tops spring back when pressed. Cool for 5 minutes, then turn out onto a cooling rack and peel off the lining paper. Allow to cool.

Make the maple frosting. Pour the maple syrup into a saucepan and heat to 240°F on a candy thermometer. As the temperature begins to rise, beat the egg whites and salt in a clean bowl until stiff. When the syrup is ready, beat it into the egg whites in a thin trickle until the frosting is like a meringue mixture. Keep beating for a few minutes more until very thick.

Cut each cake in half then sandwich 4 layers together with frosting. Transfer to a serving plate, then swirl the rest of the frosting over the top and sides of the cake. Decorate the top with the walnut pieces.

For spiced apple cake with calvados cream, make the cake omitting the orange zest, carrots, and walnuts. Add 7 oz peeled, cored, and coarsely grated cooking apples instead. Bake as above, then sandwich with ⅔ cup heavy cream, whipped and folded with 2 tablespoons calvados and 2 tablespoons honey. Dust the top with confectioners' sugar.

victoria layer cake

Cuts into **8**
Preparation time **20 minutes**
Cooking time **20 minutes**

¾ cup **butter**, at room
   temperature
¾ cup **superfine sugar**
1 cup **brown rice flour**
3 **eggs**
1 tablespoon **baking powder**
a few drops of **vanilla extract**
1 tablespoon **milk**

To decorate
4 tablespoons **raspberry jelly**
sifted confectioners' sugar,
   for dusting

Place all the cake ingredients in a mixing bowl or a
food processor and beat well until smooth.

Divide the mixture evenly between 2 greased and
floured 7 inch nonstick round cake pans and bake in
a preheated oven, 400°F, for about 20 minutes until
golden and risen.

Remove from the oven and turn out onto a cooling
rack to cool. Sandwich the cakes together with the
jelly and dust with confectioners' sugar.

For chocolate birthday cake, make the cakes above,
replacing 1 tablespoon rice flour with cocoa powder.
Make a chocolate frosting by dissolving 2 tablespoons
cocoa powder in 2 tablespoons boiling water and
allowing to cool. Beat together 3⅓ cups confectioners'
sugar and ¾ cup softened butter until pale and fluffy,
then beat in the dissolved cocoa. Use to fill and cover
the cake.

chocolate guinness cake

Cuts into **10**

Preparation time **40 minutes**, plus standing and chilling

Cooking time **45–55 minutes**

½ cup **butter**, at room temperature

1 cup **light brown sugar**

1½ cups **all-purpose flour**

½ cup **cocoa powder**

½ teaspoon **baking powder**

1 teaspoon **baking soda**

3 **eggs**, beaten

¾ cup **Guinness** or other stout

1 oz **white chocolate curls**, to decorate

sifted **cocoa powder**, for dusting

For the white chocolate frosting

¾ cup **heavy cream**

7 oz **white chocolate**, broken into pieces

Cream the butter and sugar together in a mixing bowl until pale and creamy. Sift the flour, cocoa, baking powder, and baking soda into a bowl. Gradually beat in alternate spoonfuls of egg, flour mixture, and Guinness until all have been added and the mixture is smooth.

Spoon into an 8 inch springform pan, greased and base-lined with oiled waxed paper, and spread the surface level. Bake in a preheated oven, 325°F, for 45–55 minutes until well risen, the top is slightly cracked, and a toothpick inserted into the center comes out clean. Allow to cool in the pan for 10 minutes then loosen the edges, turn out onto a cooling rack and peel off the lining paper.

Make the white chocolate frosting. Bring half the cream just to a boil in a small saucepan, then remove from the heat. Add the chocolate, set aside for 10 minutes until melted. Stir then chill for 15 minutes. Whip the remaining cream then beat in the chocolate cream until thick. Chill for another 15 minutes.

Transfer the cake to a serving plate and spoon the chocolate cream over the top. Decorate with chocolate curls and dust with sifted cocoa powder.

cherry & orange roulade

Cuts into **8**
Preparation time **30 minutes,
plus cooling**
Cooking time **20 minutes**

5 large **eggs**, separated
1 cup **superfine sugar**, plus
extra for dusting
1 cup **all-purpose flour**, sifted
grated zest of 1½ **oranges**
⅓ cup **slivered almonds**
1¼ cups **low-fat cream
cheese**
14 oz can **pitted black
cherries**, drained
a few **fresh cherries** (optional)

Put the egg yolks and ¾ cup sugar in a large heatproof bowl set over a saucepan of gently simmering water. Beat until very thick and pale. Remove from the heat and gently fold in the sifted flour and the zest from 1 orange. Beat the egg whites in a large clean bowl until stiff but moist-looking. Fold a large spoonful into the yolk mixture to loosen it slightly, then gently fold in the rest.

Pour the mixture into a 12 x 9 inch baking pan lined with nonstick parchment paper, and ease into the corners. Sprinkle with the slivered almonds and bake in a preheated oven, 350°F, for 15 minutes until the roulade is well risen and the top feels spongy. Remove from the oven and allow to cool.

Beat the cream cheese with the remaining orange zest and half the remaining sugar.

Cover a clean damp dish towel with nonstick parchment paper and sprinkle with the remaining sugar. Turn out the roulade onto the paper. Peel off the lining paper.

Spread the cream cheese mixture over the top. Sprinkle with the canned cherries then, starting with a short side and using the paper to help, roll up the roulade. Transfer to a serving plate, add fresh cherries, if using, and cut into thick slices to serve.

For passion fruit and mango gâteau, make the sponge cake omitting the orange zest and bake as above. When cooked, cut into three strips widthwise. Sandwich and top strips with 1¼ cups whipped heavy cream, the peeled, pitted, and diced flesh of 1 mango and the pulp from 3 passion fruit.

lemon cornmeal cake

Cuts into **8–10**
Preparation time **20 minutes**
Cooking time **30 minutes**

1 cup **all-purpose flour**
1½ teaspoons **baking powder**
⅔ cup **yellow cornmeal**
3 **eggs**, plus 2 **egg whites**
¾ cup **golden superfine**
   sugar
grated zest and juice of
   2 **lemons**
6 tablespoons **vegetable oil**
⅔ cup **buttermilk**

For the red wine
   strawberries
1¼ cups **red wine**
1 **vanilla bean**, split
⅔ cup **superfine sugar**
2 tablespoons **balsamic**
   vinegar
1⅔ cups **strawberries**, hulled

Sift the flour and baking powder into a mixing bowl. Stir in the cornmeal and set aside.

Beat the eggs, egg whites, and sugar together in another bowl, using an electric beater, for 3–4 minutes until pale and very thick. Fold in the cornmeal mixture, lemon zest and juice, vegetable oil, and buttermilk to form a smooth batter.

Pour the mixture into a greased and base-lined 10 inch springform cake pan. Bake in a preheated oven, 350°F, for 30 minutes until risen and firm to the touch. Allow to cool in the pan for 10 minutes then loosen the edges, turn out onto a cooling rack and peel off the lining paper. Allow to cool.

Meanwhile, prepare the red wine strawberries. Put the wine, vanilla bean, and sugar in a saucepan and heat gently to dissolve the sugar. Increase the heat and simmer for 10–15 minutes until reduced and syrupy. Allow to cool then stir in the balsamic vinegar and strawberries.

Cut the cake into slices and serve as a dessert with the strawberries and their syrup.

For lemon drizzle cake, omit the red wine accompaniment. Make the cake as above. Heat the finely grated zest and juice of 2 lemons in a saucepan with 1 cup superfine sugar and 2 tablespoons water, until the sugar has just dissolved. Turn the cooked cake out onto a plate and spoon the hot syrup over the top. Allow it to cool and to absorb the syrup. Serve cut into wedges with whipped heavy cream.

chocolate & hazelnut gâteau

Cuts into **8–10**

Preparation time **30 minutes, plus chilling**

Cooking time **1–1¼ hours**

5 **eggs**, separated
1¼ cups **superfine sugar**
1 tablespoon **cornstarch**
1 cup **blanched hazelnuts**, toasted and finely ground
cocoa powder, for dusting

For the filling
8 oz **semisweet chocolate**, broken into pieces
¾ cup **heavy cream**

For the chocolate hazelnuts
½ cup **hazelnuts**
2 oz **semisweet chocolate**, melted

Beat the egg whites in a large clean bowl until stiff. Beat in the sugar, a tablespoonful at time, until it has all been added. Beat again until the meringue mixture is thick and glossy. Fold in the cornstarch and ground hazelnuts then spoon the mixture into a large pastry bag fitted with a ½ inch plain piping tip.

Draw a 9 inch circle on 3 sheets of nonstick parchment paper. Starting in the center of each prepared circle, pipe the mixture in a continuous coil, finishing just within the outer line. Bake all 3 in a preheated oven, 300°F, for 1–1¼ hours until lightly golden and dried out. Remove from the oven and transfer to a cooling rack to cool completely.

Heat the chocolate and cream in a heatproof bowl set over a saucepan of simmering water, stirring until the chocolate has melted. Remove from the heat and allow to cool then chill for 1 hour until thickened.

Make the chocolate hazelnuts. Using a fork, dip the hazelnuts into the melted chocolate until coated. Allow to set on parchment paper.

Beat the chocolate filling until light and fluffy and use it to sandwich the 3 meringue layers together. Decorate with the chocolate hazelnuts and serve dusted with cocoa powder.

For apricot & almond dacquiose, replace the hazelnuts with ground almonds. For the filling, cover 1 cup ready-to-eat dried apricots with water and cook in a saucepan for 10 minutes. Puree until smooth, cool, then fold into 1¼ cups whipped heavy cream.

cut-&-come-again cakes

pepper cake

Cuts into **10**

Preparation time **25 minutes, plus cooling**

Cooking time **45–55 minutes**

½ cup **butter**
¾ cup **raisins**
¾ cup **currants**
½ cup **golden raisins**
⅔ cup **light brown sugar**
⅔ cup **water**
2½ cups **self-rising flour**
1 teaspoon **peppercorns,** coarsely crushed
1 teaspoon **whole cloves,** coarsely crushed
1 teaspoon **ground ginger**
2 **eggs**

Put the butter, dried fruit, sugar, and water in a saucepan and bring to a boil. Heat gently for 5 minutes then allow to cool for 15 minutes.

Put the flour, crushed peppercorns, crushed cloves, and ginger in a mixing bowl. Add the fruit mixture and eggs and mix to a soft dropping consistency.

Spoon into an 8 inch springform pan, greased and base-lined with oiled waxed paper. Spread the surface level then bake in a preheated oven, 325°F, for 45–55 minutes until well risen, the top is slightly cracked and a toothpick inserted into the center comes out clean. (If you have a fan-assisted oven, you may need to cover the top of the cake lightly with foil after 30 minutes to prevent the top from overbrowning.)

Allow to cool for 10 minutes then loosen the edges, turn out onto a cooling rack and peel off the lining paper. Allow to cool completely. Store in an airtight container for up to 3 days.

For light farmhouse fruit cake, follow the recipe above but omit the peppercorns, whole cloves, and ground ginger and add 1 teaspoon mixed spice to the mixture instead.

banana, date, & walnut loaf

Cuts into **10**
Preparation time **25 minutes**
Cooking time **1 hour 10 minutes–1¼ hours**

13 oz **bananas**, weighed with skins on
1 tablespoon **lemon juice**
2½ cups **self-rising flour**
1 teaspoon **baking powder**
½ cup **superfine sugar**
½ cup **butter**, melted
2 **eggs**, beaten
1 cup **ready-chopped dried dates**
⅓ cup **walnut pieces**

To decorate
walnut halves
banana chips

Peel then mash the bananas with the lemon juice.

Put the flour, baking powder, and sugar in a mixing bowl. Add the mashed bananas, melted butter, and eggs and mix together. Stir in the dates and walnut pieces then spoon into a greased 2 lb loaf pan, its base and 2 long sides also lined with oiled waxed paper. Spread the surface level and decorate the top with walnut halves and banana chips, if using.

Bake in the center of a preheated oven, 325°F, for 1 hour 10 minutes–1¼ hours until well risen, the top has cracked and a toothpick inserted into the center comes out clean. Allow to cool for 10 minutes then loosen the edges, turn out onto a cooling rack and peel off the lining paper. Allow to cool completely. Store in an airtight container for up to 5 days.

For chocolate, cherry, & apricot loaf, add 3 oz diced dark chocolate, ⅓ cup candied cherries, roughly chopped, and ½ cup ready-to-eat dried apricots, diced, instead of the dates and walnuts. Spoon into the loaf pan and bake as above. Drizzle the top of the cooled cake with 3 oz melted dark chocolate.

jamaican ginger cake

Cuts into **10**
Preparation time **30 minutes**
Cooking time **50–60 minutes**

⅔ cup **butter**
½ cup **corn syrup**
½ cup **molasses**
1¼ cups **all-purpose flour**
½ cup **whole-wheat bread flour**
4 teaspoons **ground ginger**
1 teaspoon **ground mixed spice**
1 teaspoon **baking soda**
2 **eggs**, beaten
4 tablespoons **milk**

For the topping
1 tablespoon **apricot jelly**
¾ cup **exotic dried fruit**, cut into strips
1 piece **stem ginger**, drained and sliced

Put the butter, syrup, and molasses in a saucepan and heat gently, stirring occasionally, until the butter has melted. Remove from the heat and cool for 5 minutes.

Mix all the dry ingredients together in a large mixing bowl. Gradually mix in the syrup mixture then the eggs and milk and beat well until smooth.

Pour into a greased 2 lb loaf pan, its base and 2 long sides also lined with oiled waxed paper. Bake in a preheated oven, 325°F, for 50–60 minutes until well risen, the top has cracked and a toothpick inserted into the center comes out clean. Allow to cool in the pan for 10 minutes then loosen the edges and lift out of the pan using the lining paper. Transfer to a cooling rack, peel off the lining paper and allow to cool.

Spread the top of the cake with the apricot jelly, then decorate with strips of exotic dried fruit and ginger.

For parkin, make the ginger cake as above, replacing the whole-wheat flour with ¾ cup medium oatmeal. Bake in an 8 inch square cake pan that has been lined with nonstick parchment paper on the base and sides. Bake at 300°F, for 50–60 minutes or until firm to the touch. When cool, turn out and wrap in waxed paper. Cut into 16 squares to serve.

whiskey mac cake

Cuts into **24**

Preparation time **40 minutes,
plus overnight soaking**

Cooking time **3½ –3¾ hours**

6 cups **luxury mixed dried
fruit**

4 tablespoons **whiskey**

⅓ cup **ready-chopped
crystallized ginger**

grated zest and juice of
1 lemon

2½ cups **all-purpose flour**

2 teaspoons **ground mixed
spice**

1 teaspoon **ground cinnamon**

1 cup **butter**, at room
temperature

1 cup **dark brown sugar**

5 **eggs**, beaten

½ cup **pecan nuts**, roughly
chopped

To decorate

11 **candied cherry halves**

11 **pecan nuts**

Put the dried fruit in a bowl with the whiskey, crystallized ginger, lemon zest, and juice. Mix together, cover, and allow to soak overnight.

Mix the flour with the spices. Beat the butter and sugar together in a mixing bowl until pale and creamy.

Mix in alternate spoonfuls of beaten egg and flour until all has been added and the mixture is smooth. Gradually mix in the soaked fruit and chopped nuts until evenly combined.

Spoon the mixture into an 8 inch deep round cake pan, base and sides lined with nonstick parchment paper, and spread the surface level. Arrange the cherry halves and pecans around the top edge. Bake in the center of a preheated oven, 275°F, for 3½–3¾ hours or until a toothpick inserted into the center comes out clean. Allow to cool in the pan for 30 minutes then loosen the edges, turn out onto a wire rack and peel off the lining paper. Allow to cool completely. Decorate the cake with a strip of waxed paper tied round the cake with raffia, if desired. Store in an airtight container for up to 2 weeks.

For rich fruit celebration cake, omit the whiskey and soak the fruit in the grated zest and juice of 1 lemon and ½ orange. Omit the cherry and pecan topping and bake as above. When cold, place the cake on a cake board and brush the top and sides with 4 tablespoons apricot jelly. Cover with 14 oz thinly rolled marzipan, then 1 lb ready-to-use icing. Smooth the top and sides and trim off any excess. Decorate to suit the celebration.

cidered apple & fig loaf

Cuts into **10**
Preparation time **20 minutes,
  plus soaking**
Cooking time **1 hour–1 hour
  10 minutes**

1¼ cups **dry hard cider**
1 large **cooking apple**, about
  10 oz in total, cored, peeled,
  and chopped
1 cup **ready-to-eat dried figs**,
  chopped
⅔ cup **superfine sugar**
2½ cups **self-rising flour**
2 **eggs**, beaten
1 tablespoon **sunflower
  seeds**
1 tablespoon **pumpkin seeds**

Pour the cider into a saucepan, add the apple and figs and bring to a boil. Simmer for 3–5 minutes until the apples are just tender but still firm. Remove the pan from the heat and allow to soak for 4 hours.

Mix the sugar, flour, and eggs into the soaked fruit and stir well.

Spoon into a greased 2 lb loaf pan, its base and 2 long sides also lined with oiled waxed paper and spread the surface level. Sprinkle with the seeds and bake in the center of a preheated oven, 325°F, for 1 hour–1 hour 10 minutes until well risen, the top has slightly cracked and a toothpick inserted into the center comes out clean.

Allow to cool in the pan for 10 minutes then loosen the edges and lift out of the pan using the lining paper. Transfer to a wire rack, peel off the lining paper, and allow to cool completely. Serve cut into slices and spread with a little butter. Store in an airtight container for up to 1 week.

For apple & mixed fruit loaf, cook the apple as above in 1¼ cups apple juice instead of hard cider with 1 cup luxury mixed dried fruit instead of dried figs. Continue as above, spooning the mixture into the pan and sprinkling the top with roughly crushed sugar cubes or leave plain if preferred.

pear, cardamom, & raisin cake

Cuts into **10**
Preparation time **20 minutes**
Cooking time **1¼–1½ hours**

½ cup **unsalted butter**, at
   room temperature
½ cup **light brown sugar**
2 **eggs**, lightly beaten
2 cups **self-rising flour**
1 teaspoon **ground
   cardamom**
4 tablespoons **milk**
1 lb **pears**, peeled, cored,
   and thinly sliced
¾ cup **golden raisins**
1 tablespoon **honey**

Beat the butter and sugar together in a mixing bowl until pale and creamy. Gradually beat in the eggs, a little at a time, until incorporated. Sift the flour and ground cardamom together and fold them into the creamed mixture with the milk.

Reserve about one-third of the pear slices and roughly chop the rest. Fold the chopped pears into the creamed mixture with the golden raisins. Spoon the mixture into a greased 2 lb loaf pan, its base and 2 long sides also lined with oiled waxed paper. Spread the surface level.

Arrange the reserved pear slices along the center of the cake, pressing them in gently. Bake in a preheated oven, 325°F, for 1¼–1½ hours or until a toothpick inserted into the center comes out clean.

Remove the cake from the oven. Allow to cool in the pan for 10 minutes then loosen the edges and lift out of the pan using the lining paper. Transfer to a cooling rack, peel off the lining paper, and allow to cool completely. Drizzle with the honey.

For date & apple ripple cake, simmer 1¼ cups ready-chopped, pitted dates in a covered saucepan with ⅔ cup water for 5 minutes until soft. Puree until smooth. Make the cake as above, but omit the cardamom, pears, golden raisins, and honey and replace them with 12 oz peeled and diced cooking apples. Spoon half the cake mixture into the cake pan, top with the date mixture and then the remaining cake mixture. Bake as above.

spiced marmalade cake

Cuts into **24**
Preparation time **25 minutes**
Cooking time **35–40 minutes**

½ cup **butter**
⅔ cup **corn syrup**
½ cup **superfine sugar**
2 tablespoons **chunky
    marmalade**
2 tablespoons **chopped
    candied peel** (optional)
2 cups **self-rising flour**
2 teaspoons **ground mixed
    spice**
1 teaspoon **ground ginger**
½ teaspoon **baking soda**
⅔ cup **milk**
2 **eggs**, beaten

For the topping
2 **oranges**, thinly sliced
¼ cup **superfine sugar**
¾ cup **water**
2 tablespoons **marmalade**

Put the butter, corn syrup, sugar, and marmalade in a saucepan and heat gently until melted.

Remove from the heat and stir in the chopped peel, if using, and the dry ingredients. Add the milk and beaten eggs and mix until smooth. Pour into an 8 inch deep square cake pan, greased and base-lined with oiled waxed paper. Bake in a preheated oven, 350°F, for 35–40 minutes until well risen and a toothpick inserted into the center comes out clean.

Meanwhile, put the sliced oranges into a saucepan with the sugar and water. Cover and simmer for 25 minutes until tender. Remove the lid and cook for 5 minutes more, until the liquid has been reduced to about 2 tablespoons. Add the marmalade and heat until melted.

Allow the cake to cool in the pan for 10 minutes then loosen the edges, turn out onto a cooling rack and peel off the lining paper. Turn the cake the right way up and spoon over the oranges and sauce. Store in an airtight container for up to 3 days.

For light pecan gingerbread, omit the marmalade from the recipe and add 3 teaspoons ground ginger instead of the mixture of ginger and mixed spice. Stir in ⅓ cup halved pecan nuts, then pour into the cake pan and bake as above. Omit the topping.

dundee cake

Cuts into **12–14**
Preparation time **30 minutes**
Cooking time **1¾–2 hours**

2 cups **all-purpose flour**
1 teaspoon **baking powder**
1 teaspoon **mixed spice**
½ cup **ground almonds**
grated zest and juice of
  ½ **lemon**
¾ cup **butter**, at room
  temperature
¾ cup **light brown sugar**
4 **eggs**, beaten
3 cups **luxury mixed dried
  fruit**
2½ tablespoons **blanched
  almonds**

Mix the flour, baking powder, spice, ground almonds, and lemon zest together in a bowl.

Beat the butter and sugar together in another bowl until pale and creamy. Gradually mix in alternate spoonfuls of beaten egg and flour mixture until all has been added and the mixture is smooth. Stir in the dried fruit and the lemon juice.

Spoon the mixture into an 8 inch deep round cake pan lined base and sides with nonstick parchment paper. Spread the surface level and arrange the almonds in rings over the top. Bake in a preheated oven, 325°F, for 1¾–2 hours until a deep brown and a toothpick inserted into the center comes out clean. Check the cake after 1 hour and cover loosely with foil if the almonds look as though they are going to overbrown.

Allow to cool in the pan for 15 minutes then loosen the edges, turn out onto a cooling rack and peel off the lining paper. Allow to cool completely. Store in an airtight container for up to 1 week.

For Easter simnel cake, make the cake mixture as above and spoon half of it into the pan and spread level. Roll out 6 oz yellow marzipan to the same size as the pan and press onto the cake mixture. Top with the remaining cake mixture. Omit the nut topping and bake as above. To finish, brush the top of the cake with 1 tablespoon apricot jelly then cover with 6 oz rolled marzipan to fit the top. Crimp the edges and brown lightly under the broiler.

tropical christmas cake

Cuts into **10**
Preparation time **30 minutes**
Cooking time 1¼ –1½ **hours**

1¼ cups **unsalted butter**, at
  room temperature
1 cup **superfine sugar**
3 large **eggs**, beaten
3½ cups **self-rising flour**,
  sifted
⅓ cup **candied cherries**,
⅓ cup **mixed peel**
3 tablespoons **angelica**
3 tablespoons **walnuts**
8 oz can **pineapple rings in
  syrup**, drained and the
  syrup reserved
3 tablespoons **shredded
  coconut**
½ cup **golden raisins**
2 tablespoons toasted
  coconut shavings,
  to decorate

For the frosting
2⅓ cups **confectioners' sugar**
3 tablespoons **unsalted
  butter**, melted
2 tablespoons **shredded
  coconut**

Beat the butter and sugar together in a bowl until pale and creamy. Gradually mix in alternate spoonfuls of beaten egg and flour until all has been added.

Chop the dried fruit, nuts, and pineapple and then fold into the cake mixture with the coconut, golden raisins, and 3 tablespoons of the reserved pineapple syrup.

Spoon the mixture into a greased and floured 9 inch tube pan or 8 inch cake pan. Bake in a preheated oven, 325°F, for 1¼ hours if using a tube pan and 1½ hours if using a cake pan. Allow to cool in the pan for at least 10 minutes then loosen the edges and turn out onto a cooling rack. Allow to cool completely.

Make the frosting. Sift the confectioners' sugar into the melted butter, then add 1 tablespoon of the reserved pineapple syrup and the coconut. Stir to combine, then spread the frosting over the top of the cake and a little down the sides. Sprinkle with toasted coconut shavings to decorate.

For paradise cake, replace the pineapple juice with 3 tablespoons dark rum in the cake mixture and continue as above. Decorate the top of the cooked cake with a rich, dark chocolate frosting made by heating 2 tablespoons butter and 4 oz semisweet chocolate gently in a pan. Mix in 3 tablespoons confectioners' sugar and 2–3 teaspoons milk to make a smooth spoonable frosting. Spoon over the top of the cake and decorate with extra angelica and candied cherries.

198

cranberry & cherry cake

Cuts into **12**
Preparation time **30 minutes**
Cooking time **1 hour 10
    minutes–1 hour 20 minutes**

1 cup **candied cherries**
¾ cup **butter**, at room
    temperature
¾ cup **superfine sugar**
grated zest of 1 small **orange**
3 **eggs**, beaten
1¾ cups **self-rising flour**
½ cup **dried cranberries**
a few **sugar cubes**, roughly
    crushed, to decorate

Put the cherries in a sieve, rinse with cold water then drain and pat dry with paper towels. (This ensures they don't sink during cooking.) Halve ¼ cup and reserve for decoration. Roughly chop the remainder.

Beat the butter and sugar together in a mixing bowl or a food processor until pale and creamy. Stir in the orange zest then gradually mix in alternate spoonfuls of beaten egg and flour until all has been added and the mixture is smooth.

Fold in the chopped candied cherries and cranberries. Spoon the mixture into a 7 inch deep round cake pan lined base and sides with nonstick parchment paper. Spread the surface level then lightly press the reserved halved cherries into the cake mixture and sprinkle with the crushed sugar cubes.

Bake in a preheated oven, 325°F, for about 1 hour 10 minutes–1 hour 20 minutes until well risen, the top is golden brown and a toothpick inserted into the center comes out clean.

Allow to cool in the pan for 10 minutes then loosen the edges, turn out onto a cooling rack and peel off the lining paper. Allow to cool completely. Store in an airtight container for up to 5 days.

For date & apricot cake, omit the cherries and cranberries and add ½ cup roughly chopped pitted dates and ½ cup chopped ready-to-eat dried apricots. Bake as above, leaving the top of the cake plain.

lemon & poppy seed cake

Cuts into **10**

Preparation time **25 minutes**

Cooking time **1 hour–1 hour 10 minutes**

¾ cup **butter**, at room temperature

¾ cup **superfine sugar**

3 **eggs**, beaten

2 cups **self-rising flour**

1 teaspoon **baking powder**

¼ cup **poppy seeds**

grated zest and juice of 2 **lemons**

To finish

1 cup **confectioners' sugar**

3–4 teaspoons **lemon juice**

citron peel, cut into thin strips

Beat the butter and sugar together in a mixing bowl until pale and creamy. Gradually mix in alternate spoonfuls of beaten egg and flour until all has been added and the mixture is smooth. Stir in the baking powder, poppy seeds, lemon zest, and 5–6 tablespoons lemon juice to make a soft dropping consistency.

Spoon the mixture into a greased 2 lb loaf pan, its base and 2 long sides also lined with oiled waxed paper. Spread the surface level and bake in a preheated oven, 325°F, for 1 hour–1 hour 10 minutes until well risen, the top is cracked and golden and a toothpick inserted into the center comes out clean.

Allow to cool in the pan for 10 minutes then loosen the edges and lift out of the pan using the lining paper. Transfer to a cooling rack, peel off the lining paper, and allow to cool.

Sift the confectioners' sugar into a bowl then gradually mix in enough of the lemon juice to make a smooth coating icing. Drizzle over the top of the cake in random squiggly lines. Add strips of peel to the top and allow to set. Store in an airtight container for up to 1 week.

For orange & caraway cake, follow the recipe above but replace the poppy seeds and lemon with 1½ teaspoons roughly crushed caraway seeds, the grated zest of 1 large orange, and 5–6 tablespoons orange juice. Decorate the top of the cake with 1½ tablespoons roughly crushed sugar lumps before baking and omit the lemon icing.

apricot tea bread

Cuts into **10**
Preparation time **25 minutes,**
  plus soaking
Cooking time **1 hour**

⅔ cup **ready-to-eat dried**
  apricots, chopped
⅔ cup **golden raisins**
⅔ cup **raisins**
⅔ cup **superfine sugar**
1¼ cups **hot strong tea**
2¼ cups **self-rising flour**
1 teaspoon **baking soda**
1 teaspoon **ground cinnamon**
1 **egg**, beaten

Put the dried fruits and sugar in a mixing bowl, add the hot tea and mix together. Allow to soak for 4 hours or overnight.

Mix the flour, baking soda, and cinnamon together, add to the soaked fruit with the beaten egg and mix together well.

Spoon into a greased 2 lb loaf pan, its base and 2 long sides also lined with oiled waxed paper. Spread the surface level then bake in the center of a preheated oven, 325°F, for about 1 hour until well risen, the top has cracked and a toothpick inserted into the center comes out clean.

Allow to cool in the pan for 10 minutes then loosen the edges and lift out of the pan using the lining paper. Transfer to a cooling rack, peel off the lining paper, and allow to cool completely. Cut into slices and spread with a little butter to serve. Store, unbuttered, in an airtight container for up to 1 week.

For prune & orange bread, use 1 cup ready-to-eat, pitted prunes, chopped, instead of the apricots and golden raisins, and increase the quantity of raisins to ¾ cup. Mix with the superfine sugar as above, add the grated zest of 1 orange, then soak in ⅔ cup orange juice and ⅔ cup boiling water instead of the tea. Add the flour, baking soda, and beaten egg as above, omitting the cinnamon. Spoon into a loaf pan and continue the recipe as above.

pastries

citrus baklava

Makes **24**

Preparation time **30 minutes,
    plus chilling**

Cooking time **35–40 minutes**

13 oz package **frozen phyllo
    pastry**, defrosted

½ cup **butter**, melted

For the filling

⅔ cup **walnut pieces**

1 cup **shelled pistachio nuts**

¾ cup **blanched almonds**

⅓ cup **superfine sugar**

½ teaspoon **ground cinnamon**

For the syrup

1 **lemon**

1 small **orange**

1 cup **superfine sugar**

pinch of **ground cinnamon**

⅔ cup **water**

To decorate

few slivers **pistachio nuts**

Dry-fry the nuts in a nonstick pan for 3–4 minutes, stirring until lightly browned. Allow to cool slightly then roughly chop and mix with the sugar and spice.

Unfold the pastry and cut it into rectangles the same size as the base of a 7 x 11 inch small roasting pan. Wrap half the pastry in plastic wrap so that it doesn't dry out. Brush each unwrapped sheet of pastry with melted butter then layer up in the roasting pan. Spoon in the nut mixture then unwrap and cover with the remaining pastry, buttering layers as you go.

Cut the pastry into 6 squares, then cut each square into 4 triangles. Bake in a preheated oven, 350°F, for 30–35 minutes, covering with foil after 20 minutes to prevent it overbrowning.

Meanwhile, make the syrup. Pare the peel off the citrus fruits with a zester or vegetable peeler then cut the peel into strips. Squeeze the juice. Put the strips and juice in a saucepan with the sugar, cinnamon, and water. Heat gently until the sugar dissolves then simmer for 5 minutes without stirring.

Pour the hot syrup over the pastry as soon as it comes out of the oven. Allow to cool, then chill for 3 hours. Remove from the pan and arrange the pieces on a serving plate, sprinkled with slivers of pistachio. Store in the refrigerator for up to 2 days.

For rose water baklava, omit the orange peel and juice from the syrup and add 4 tablespoons extra water and 1 tablespoon rose water, or to taste. Pour over the cooked baklava and finish as above.

208

french apple flan

Makes **4**

Preparation time **20 minutes,
plus chilling**

Cooking time **25–30 minutes**

12 oz **ready-made puff
pastry**

2 **crisp green dessert apples**
(such as Granny Smith),
peeled, cored, and sliced

1 tablespoon **superfine sugar**

2 tablespoons **unsalted
butter**, chilled

ice cream, to serve

For the apricot glaze

1 cup **apricot jam**

2 teaspoons **lemon juice**

2 teaspoons **water**

Divide the pastry into quarters and roll each out on a lightly floured surface until ⅛ inch thick. Using a 5½ inch plate as a guide, cut out 4 rounds—make a number of short cuts around the plate rather than drawing the knife around, which can stretch the pastry. Place the rounds on a cookie sheet.

Place a slightly smaller plate on each pastry round and score around the edge to form a ½ inch border. Prick the centers with a fork and chill for 30 minutes.

Arrange the apple slices in a circle over the pastry rounds and sprinkle with the sugar. Grate the butter over the top and bake in a preheated oven, 425°F, for 25–30 minutes until the pastry and apples are golden.

Meanwhile, make the apricot glaze. Put the jam in a small saucepan with the lemon juice and water and heat gently until the jam melts. Increase the heat and boil for 1 minute, remove from the heat and press through a fine sieve. Keep warm then brush over each apple tart while they are still warm. Serve with ice cream.

For peach tartlets, replace the 2 apples with 2 peaches, halved, skinned, and thinly sliced. Arrange on the pastry rounds and continue as above, baking for 12–15 minutes.

chocolate éclairs with cream liqueur

Makes **18**
Preparation time **40 minutes, plus cooling**
Cooking time **15 minutes**

⅔ cup **water**
¼ cup **butter**
½ cup **all-purpose flour**, sifted
2 **eggs**, beaten
½ teaspoon **vanilla extract**

For the filling

1 cup **heavy cream**
2 tablespoons **confectioners' sugar**
4 tablespoons **whiskey and coffee cream liqueur** (such as Baileys)

For the topping

2 tablespoons **butter**
4 oz **semisweet chocolate**, broken into pieces
1 tablespoon **confectioners' sugar**
2–3 teaspoons **milk**

Heat the water and butter gently in a saucepan until melted. Bring to a boil then add the flour and beat until it forms a smooth ball that leaves the sides of the pan almost clean. Allow to cool for 10 minutes.

Gradually mix in the eggs and vanilla until thick and smooth. Spoon the choux mixture into a large nylon pastry bag fitted with a ½ inch plain piping tip and pipe 3 inch lines of mixture onto a large lightly greased cookie sheet.

Bake in a preheated oven, 400°F, for 15 minutes until well risen. Make a slit in the side of each éclair for the steam to escape then return to the turned-off oven for 5 minutes. Allow to cool.

Whip the cream to soft swirls then gradually beat in the confectioners' sugar and liqueur. Slit each éclair lengthwise and spoon or pipe in the cream.

Make the chocolate topping. Heat the butter, chocolate, and confectioners' sugar together gently until just melted. Stir in the milk then spoon over the top of the éclairs. Serve the same day.

For chocolate profiteroles, pipe small balls of the choux mixture onto cookie sheets. Bake as above for 10–12 minutes. When cool, fill with plain whipped cream and drizzle with a smooth chocolate sauce made by gently heating 5 oz semisweet chocolate with 1 tablespoon butter, 2 tablespoons superfine sugar and ⅔ cup milk.

raspberry garlands

Makes **8**
Preparation time **30 minutes,**
  plus cooling
Cooking time **15 minutes**

⅔ cup **water**
¼ cup **butter**
½ cup **all-purpose flour**, sifted
2 **eggs**, beaten
½ teaspoon **vanilla extract**
2 tablespoons **slivered**
  almonds
sifted **confectioners' sugar,**
  for dusting

For the filling
1¼ cups **full-fat sour cream**
3 tablespoons **confectioners'**
  sugar, sifted
2 cups **fresh raspberries**

Heat the water and butter gently in a saucepan until melted. Bring to a boil then add the flour and beat until it forms a smooth ball that leaves the sides of the pan almost clean. Allow to cool for 10 minutes.

Gradually mix in the eggs and vanilla until thick and smooth. Spoon the choux mixture into a large nylon pastry bag fitted with a ½ inch plain piping tip and pipe 3 inch diameter circles on a greased cookie sheet.

Sprinkle with the slivered almonds then bake in a preheated oven, 400°F, for 15 minutes. Make a small slit in the side of each choux ring for the steam to escape then return to the turned-off oven for 5 minutes. Allow to cool.

Slit each choux ring and fill with sour cream mixed with half the confectioners' sugar then sprinkle with the raspberries. Arrange on a serving plate and dust with the remaining confectioners' sugar. These are best eaten on the day they are made.

For strawberry cream puffs, make the choux pastry as above and pipe 8 choux balls onto a greased cookie sheet. Bake as above until crisp then fill the puffs with ⅔ cup plain yogurt mixed with ⅔ cup whipped heavy cream sweetened with 2 tablespoons confectioners' sugar and 1 cup sliced strawberries. Dust the tops with sifted confectioners' sugar.

baby banana & peach strudels

Makes **8**
Preparation time **30 minutes**
Cooking time **15–18 minutes**

2 **bananas**, about 6 oz each
    with skin on, peeled and
    chopped
2 tablespoons fresh **lemon
    juice**
2 small **ripe peaches**, about
    3 oz each, halved, pitted, and
    sliced
1 cup **blueberries**
2 tablespoons **superfine
    sugar**
2 tablespoons **fresh bread
    crumbs**
½ teaspoon **ground cinnamon**
9 oz package 6 **phyllo pastry
    sheets**, defrosted if frozen
¼ cup **butter**, melted
sifted **confectioners' sugar**,
    for dusting

Toss the bananas in the lemon juice then place in a
large bowl with the peach slices and blueberries. Mix
the sugar, bread crumbs, and cinnamon in a small bowl
then gently mix with the fruit.

Unfold the pastry sheets, put one in front of you with
the longest edge nearest you.

Cut in half to make 2 rectangles, 9 x 10 inches. Put
2 heaping spoonfuls of the fruit mixture on each then
fold in the sides, brush the pastry with a little of the
melted butter, then roll up like a parcel. Repeat to make
8 mini strudels using 4 sheets of pastry.

Brush the strudels with a little more melted butter. Cut
the remaining pastry sheets into wide strips then wrap
them like bandages around the strudels, covering any
tears or splits in the pastry. Place on an ungreased
baking sheet and brush with the remaining butter.

Bake in a preheated oven, 375°F, for 15–18 minutes
until golden brown and crisp. Allow to cool on the
baking sheet then dust with a little sifted confectioners'
sugar and arrange on a serving plate. These are best
eaten on the day they are made.

For traditional apple strudels, replace the bananas
and peaches with 1 lb cored, peeled, and sliced
cooking apples tossed with 2 tablespoons lemon juice
and mixed with ⅓ cup golden raisins. Use ground
almonds instead of the bread crumbs and combine
with the cinnamon. Increase the quantity of sugar
to ¼ cup and continue the recipe as above.

classic lemon tart

Cuts into **8**

Preparation time **20 minutes, plus chilling**

Cooking time **40–45 minutes**

1¾ cups **all-purpose flour**
½ teaspoon **salt**
½ cup **butter**, diced
2 tablespoons **confectioners' sugar**, plus extra for dusting
2 **egg yolks**
1–2 teaspoons **cold water**

For the filling
3 **eggs**, plus 1 **egg yolk**
2 cups **heavy cream**
½ cup **sugar**
⅔ cup **lemon juice**

Put the flour and salt in a mixing bowl. Add the butter and blend with your fingertips until the mixture resembles fine bread crumbs.

Stir in the confectioners' sugar and gradually work in the egg yolks and water to make a firm dough.

Knead the dough briefly on a lightly floured surface, then cover with plastic wrap and chill for 30 minutes. Roll out the dough and use to line a 10 inch fluted pie dish or tart pan. Prick the pie shell with a fork and chill for 20 minutes.

Line the pie shell with parchment paper and ceramic pie weights and bake in a preheated oven, 400°F, for 10 minutes. Remove the paper and weights and bake for an additional 10 minutes until crisp and golden. Remove from the oven and reduce the temperature to 300°F.

Beat together all the filling ingredients, pour them into the pie shell, and bake for 20–25 minutes, or until the filling is just set. Let the tart cool completely, dust with sifted confectioners' sugar, and serve.

For dark chocolate tart, make the tart base as above and bake blind. Heat 2 cups heavy cream in a saucepan with 5 oz semisweet chocolate, stirring until the chocolate has melted. Beat 3 eggs and 1 egg yolk with ¼ cup superfine sugar and ¼ teaspoon ground cinnamon. Gradually beat in the chocolate cream. Bake as above and serve cold, dusted with sifted cocoa powder.

custard cream berry slices

Makes **8**
Preparation time **40 minutes**
Cooking time **13–16 minutes**

12 oz package **frozen puff
pastry**, defrosted
1 cup **heavy cream**
⅔ cup **ready-made custard**
1¾ cups **strawberries**, sliced
1¼ cups **raspberries**
confectioners' sugar, sifted,
optional

Roll out the pastry on a lightly floured surface and cut into 2 strips, 4 x 12 inches. Space apart on a wetted baking sheet. Prick with a fork and bake in a preheated oven, 425°F, for 10–12 minutes until well risen.

Slice each strip in half horizontally, lift off the tops and place, baked side downwards, on a separate baking sheet. Bake all strips for 3–4 minutes more to dry out the soft centers. Allow to cool.

Whip the cream then fold in the custard and spoon over 3 of the pastry strips. Arrange the strawberries and raspberries on top of each strip and then assemble. Add the last pastry slice, if desired, and dust with confectioners' sugar. Transfer to a large serving plate. Cut each custard slice into 4 to serve. These are best eaten on the day they are made.

For coffee cream slices, cook the pastry as above. Dissolve 3 teaspoons instant coffee in 2 teaspoons boiling water. Stir into the cream and custard mix. Use to sandwich the pastry strips together, omitting the summer berries. Add the fourth pastry layer and drizzle with the topping from the Chocolate éclairs with cream liqueur on page 212, and a few chocolate curls to decorate.

no-bake
cakes

cheat's lemon dainties

Cuts into **9**
Preparation time **25 minutes,
   plus chilling**

8 **sponge cake pieces**, sliced
   in half horizontally to give
   shallower pieces
½ cup **butter**, at room
   temperature
½ cup **superfine sugar**
grated zest of 2 **lemons**
2 **eggs**, separated
⅔ cup **heavy cream**
juice of 1 **lemon**

To finish
4 tablespoons **confectioners'
   sugar**
1 cup **fresh raspberries**
1 cup **blueberries**
fresh mint leaves

Line an 8 inch shallow square cake pan with plastic wrap. Arrange half of the sponge cakes in a single layer in the base of the pan.

Beat the butter, sugar, and lemon zest together until pale and creamy. Gradually beat in the egg yolks.

Beat the egg whites in a large clean bowl until stiff, then whip the cream in a separate bowl. Fold the whipped cream then the egg whites into the creamed mixture. Gradually fold in the juice of ½ lemon.

Drizzle a little of the remaining lemon juice over the sponge cakes. Spoon the cream mixture on top and gently spread the surface level. Cover with a second layer of sponge slices, press them gently into the cream mixture and drizzle with the remaining lemon juice. Cover with an extra piece of plastic wrap and chill in the refrigerator for 4 hours or overnight.

Remove the top layer of plastic wrap, invert the cake on to a cutting board, and peel off the remaining plastic wrap. Decorate with berries and mint leaves, dusting the tops with confectioners' sugar. Eat within 2 days of making, store in the refrigerator.

For tiramisu squares, mix 4 tablespoons strong black coffee with 2 tablespoons sherry. Spoon half over the sponge cakes in the pan. Beat 1 cup mascarpone cheese with ¼ cup superfine sugar and ⅔ cup heavy cream. Spoon half into the pan, sprinkle with 2 oz chopped dark chocolate, then repeat the layering with the rest of the ingredients and the same amount of chocolate sprinkled over the top. Chill before serving.

sicilian cheesecake

Cuts into **8**

Preparation time **20 minutes,
plus chilling**

1 cup **ricotta cheese**
½ cup **confectioners' sugar**
  (no need to sift)
⅔ cup **heavy cream**
4 oz **semisweet chocolate,**
  finely chopped
½ cup **ready-to-eat dried
  apricots,** finely chopped
⅓ cup **multicolored candied
  cherries,** roughly chopped
2 tablespoons **chopped
  candied peel**
10 **sponge cake pieces**
6 tablespoons **white rum**
cocoa powder, to decorate

Mix the ricotta cheese with the confectioners' sugar. Whip the cream until it forms soft swirls then fold into the ricotta. Reserve a few pieces of the chopped chocolate, apricots, cherries, and candied peel and fold the rest into the ricotta mixture.

Line a 7 inch deep round cake pan with 2 pieces of plastic wrap so that the base and sides are covered. Arrange half the sponge cakes over the base of the cake pan, trimming to fit. Moisten with half the rum.

Spoon two-thirds of the ricotta mixture over the sponge cakes and spread the surface level. Cover with the remaining cakes and moisten with the remaining rum. Spread the rest of the ricotta mixture on top and sprinkle with the reserved chocolate and fruits, dust with cocoa powder. Chill for 4 hours or overnight.

Loosen the edges and lift the cake out of the pan using the plastic wrap. Peel off the wrap and transfer to a serving plate. Cut into thin wedges to serve. Store in the refrigerator for up to 2 days.

For cherry kirsch gâteau, line the wrap-lined pan with sponge cakes but soak them in kirsch rather than rum. Top with a sweetened mascarpone cheese cream, rather than a ricotta cheese mixture, speckled with chopped chocolate, as above, plus a 14 oz can pitted black cherries, drained and roughly chopped, instead of the dried fruit.

layered nutty bars

Cuts into **10**
Preparation time **20 minutes,**
  plus chilling
Cooking time **5 minutes**

¼ cup **butter**
1¼ cups **fat-free sweetened**
  condensed milk
7 oz **semisweet chocolate**,
  broken into pieces
4 oz **graham crackers**
½ cup **hazelnuts**
¾ cup **shelled pistachio nuts**

Use a little of the butter to grease the base and sides of an 8 inch round springform pan. Put the rest of the butter in a saucepan with the condensed milk and chocolate. Heat gently for 3–4 minutes, stirring until melted, then remove from the heat.

Place the crackers in a plastic bag and crush roughly into chunky pieces using a rolling pin. Toast the hazelnuts under a preheated hot broiler until lightly browned, then roughly chop with the pistachios.

Stir the crackers into the chocolate mixture then spoon half the mixture into the prepared pan and spread level. Reserve 2 tablespoons of the nuts for the top, then sprinkle the rest over the chocolate layer. Cover with the remaining chocolate mixture, level the surface with the back of the spoon, and sprinkle with the reserved nuts.

Chill the nut mixture for 3–4 hours until firm, then loosen the edges and remove the sides of the pan. Cut into 10 thin slices, or into tiny bite-size pieces to make petits fours. Store any leftovers in the refrigerator, wrapped in foil, for up to 3 days.

For gingered fruit bars, make the chocolate mix as above. Omit the nuts and use ⅓ cup roughly chopped ready-to-eat dried apricots and 2 tablespoons chopped crystallized ginger, keeping 2–3 tablespoons back for the topping.

diplomatico

Cuts into **8**

Preparation time **25 minutes, plus chilling**

7 oz **semisweet chocolate**, broken into pieces

1¼ cups **heavy cream**

3 tablespoons **confectioners' sugar** (no need to sift)

4 tablespoons **brandy** or **coffee liqueur**

6 tablespoons **strong black coffee**, cooled

30 **ladyfingers**

To decorate

⅔ cup **heavy cream**

cocoa powder, sifted

Melt the chocolate in a heatproof bowl set over a saucepan of gently simmering water. Meanwhile, line a 2 lb loaf pan with plastic wrap so that the base and sides are covered.

Whip the cream until softly peaking. Fold in the confectioners' sugar then the melted chocolate. Spoon a thin layer into the base of the lined pan.

Mix the brandy or coffee liqueur and cooled coffee in a shallow dish. Dip the ladyfingers, one at a time, into the mixture to moisten then arrange in a single layer on top of the chocolate cream in the pan. Cover with half the remaining cream, then a second layer of dipped ladyfingers. Repeat the layers until all the cream and ladyfingers have been used.

Chill for 4 hours or overnight if preferred. To serve, loosen the edges and invert onto a serving plate. Peel off the plastic wrap. Whip the heavy cream and spoon over the top, then dust with cocoa powder. Cut into thick slices to serve. Refrigerate for up to 2 days.

For tiramisu, sweeten 1 cup mascarpone cheese with 2 tablespoons confectioners' sugar and mix with ⅔ cup whipped heavy cream. Layer in the lined loaf pan as above with coffee liqueur and coffee-dipped ladyfingers. Decorate with chocolate curls.

chocolate yum yums

Cuts into **15**

Preparation time **15 minutes,
  plus chilling**

5 oz **semisweet chocolate**,
  broken into pieces
½ cup **crunchy peanut butter**
2 tablespoons **butter**
2 tablespoons **corn syrup**
5 oz **graham crackers**
⅓ cup **almonds or cashew
  nuts**
sugar-coated almonds,
  roughly chopped, to
  decorate

Put the chocolate, peanut butter, butter, and syrup in a saucepan and heat gently until melted, stirring occasionally. Remove from the heat.

Place the crackers in a plastic bag and crush roughly using a rolling pin. Stir the crushed crackers and the nuts into the chocolate and stir until evenly coated.

Spoon the mixture into an 8 inch shallow square cake pan lined with nonstick parchment paper, and spread the surface level. Chill for 4 hours until firm. Lift the cake out of the pan using the lining paper, cut into 15 small squares and peel off the paper. Decorate with sugared almonds. Store in an airtight container for up to 3 days.

For chocolate marshmallow wedges, omit the peanut butter, nuts, and sugar-coated almonds. Melt the chocolate with ⅓ cup butter and ¼ cup corn syrup. Cool slightly then stir in ½ cup roughly chopped ladyfingers, ⅓ cup roughly chopped candied cherries and 2 cups mini marshmallows. Spoon into an 8 inch round pan lined with plastic wrap and sprinkle the top with ½ cup halved mini marshmallows. Chill as above. Remove from the pan, peel off the plastic wrap and cut into thin wedges.

cornflake crunchies

Makes **20**
Preparation time **15 minutes,
 plus chilling**

7 oz **semisweet chocolate,**
 broken into pieces
¼ cup **butter**
3 tablespoons **corn syrup**
4 cups **cornflakes**
mini marshmallows, sliced,
 to decorate

Place the chocolate in a saucepan with the butter and corn syrup. Heat gently, stirring occasionally, until the chocolate and butter have completely melted and the mixture is smooth and glossy.

Stir in the cornflakes and mix until completely coated in the chocolate. Spoon the cornflake mixture into 20 paper bake cups arranged on a tray or baking sheet and chill for 2–3 hours until firm. Decorate with sliced mini marshmallows.

For chocolate orange crispie cakes, follow the recipe above but replace the cornflakes with the same quantity of puffed rice cereal and adding the grated zest of 1 small orange. Finish as above.

index

acknowledgments

Executive Editor: Nicola Hill
Editor: Ruth Wiseall
Executive Art Editor: Darren Southern
Designer: Martin Topping 'ome Design
Photographer: William Shaw
Home Economist: Sara Lewis
Food and Props Stylist: Liz Hippisley
Senior Production Controller: Manjit Sihra

Special photography: © Octopus Publishing Group Ltd/William Shaw.
Other photography: © Octopus Publishing Group Ltd/Stephen Conroy 19, 69, 145; /William Lingwood 25, 41, 61, 85, 93, 97, 157, 161, 165, 177, 179, 193, 211; /Emma Neish 133, 139, 171; /Lis Parsons 33, 73, 77, 81, 89, 149, 199, 219, 229; /Gareth Sambidge 103; /Ian Wallace 141, 175.